Environments
and
Peoples

PRENTICE-HALL

Foundations of Cultural Geography Series

PHILIP L. WAGNER, *Editor*

RURAL LANDSCAPES OF THE NONWESTERN WORLD,
James M. Blaut

RURAL LANDSCAPES OF THE WESTERN WORLD,
John Fraser Hart

GEOGRAPHY OF DOMESTICATION, *Erich Isaac*

FRONTIERS OF POLITICAL GEOGRAPHY, *Roger E. Kasperson*

CULTURAL ECOLOGY, *Marvin W. Mikesell*

MIGRATION AND DIFFUSION, *Forrest R. Pitts*

HOUSING AND HOUSE FORM, *Amos Rapoport*

GEOGRAPHY OF RELIGIONS, *David E. Sopher*

GEOGRAPHY OF CITIES, *James E. Vance, Jr.*

ENVIRONMENTS AND PEOPLES, *Philip L. Wagner*

CULTURAL GEOGRAPHY OF THE UNITED STATES,
Wilbur Zelinsky

A PROLOGUE TO POPULATION GEOGRAPHY, *Wilbur Zelinsky* *

---

* *In Prentice-Hall's Foundations of Economic Geography Series, also.*

Foundations of Cultural Geography Series

Environments
and
Peoples

PHILIP L. WAGNER

Simon Fraser University

PRENTICE-HALL, INC., Englewood Cliffs, N.J.

Library of Congress Catalog Card No.: 73–173595

Current printing (last number):
10   9   8   7   6   5   4   3   2   1

C–13–283267–4
P–13–283259–3

PRENTICE-HALL INTERNATIONAL, INC., *London*
PRENTICE-HALL OF AUSTRALIA, PTY. LTD., *Sydney*
PRENTICE-HALL OF CANADA, LTD., *Toronto*
PRENTICE-HALL OF INDIA PRIVATE LIMITED, *New Delhi*
PRENTICE-HALL OF JAPAN, INC., *Tokyo*

Foundations of Cultural Geography Series

The title of this series, Foundations of Cultural Geography, represents its purpose well. Our huge and highly variegated store of knowledge about the ways that humans occupy and use their world becomes most meaningful when studied in the light of certain basic questions. Original studies of such basic questions make up this series of books by leading scholars in the field.

The authors of the series report and evaluate current thought centered on the questions: How do widely different systems of ideas and practice influence what people do to recreate and utilize their habitats? How do such systems of thought and habitat spread and evolve? How do human efforts actually change environments, and with what effects?

These questions are approached comparatively, respecting the great range of choice and experience available to mankind. They are treated historically as well, to trace and interpret and assess what man has done at various times and places. They are studied functionally, too, and whatever controlling processes and relationships they may reveal are sought.

Diverse tastes and talents govern the authors' attack on these problems. One deals with religion as a system of ideas both influencing and reflecting environmental conditions. Another evaluates the role of belief and custom in reshaping plant and animal species to human purposes. Some consider the use and meaning of human creations, like houses or cities, in geographic context; others treat of the subtle and complex relationships with nature found in agricultural systems of many sorts. One author looks at an entire country as a culturally-shaped environment; another analyzes the mechanics of the spread of customs and beliefs in space. All work toward an understanding of the same key problems. We invite the reader to participate actively in the critical rethinking by which scholarship moves forward.

PHILIP L. WAGNER

vii

to my parents, in gratitude and admiration

Preface

A fair chance now exists for man to bring about his own extinction and the ruin of the world. Still ignorant of both the consequences of his own initiatives and the inherent limitations of environments within which he must operate, man only now begins to recognize his peril. But even today, when the first alarms are sounded, no greater clarity or depth of understanding comes to reassure us, much less a clear and general agreement on any urgent measures necessary for survival.

The technological and, to a certain extent, the sociological dimensions of environmental risk and crisis have attracted some attention. Many more or less immediate ingredients of the problem have long been recognized: population pressures, resource scarcities, defective public hygiene, and technological backwardness in the "less developed" countries, and simultaneously gross environmental abuse along with a growing frustration and anomie among the peoples of the more developed nations. But we have so far no clear perception of the fundamental mechanism responsible for this dual set of symptoms. It appears that when man's peerless power to remake his world is not employed sufficiently, then multitudes are doomed to starve or sicken; at the same time, it seems that where all that power is most fully used, the habitat degenerates, and the soul itself must sicken and society be riven and demoralized. The greatest biological peculiarity of mankind, and what had previously appeared to be its greatest biological advantage—namely, the capacity of human beings to work together to transform environments—seems loaded now with tragic portent.

Geography, the study of the earth as man inhabits it, affords a special insight into mankind's plight. Comparing all the earth's diverse societies in all their varied homelands, it can hardly fail to comment on the relative success or failure of their management of the environment. Geography records a wealth of object lessons in these matters. Its perspective has to be both wider and less manageable than that, for instance, of ecology alone, for it has to take account of mankind's spatial continuities as well as of the local circumstances of each human nucleus. This need to take as it were a dual view of mankind precludes the study of human settlements as closed systems, and vitiates attempts to state precise determinant relationships within them; thus far it has inhibited geographers' attempts to formulate a viable "ecology of man." On the other hand, a dual view encompasses a larger range of influential factors, consistent with the true dimensions of the problem as we know them to exist in practice. But given even such a broad perspective, or perhaps because of it, geography's precocious sense of crisis until now has only led to feeble outcries, scarcely heard beyond the discipline's small ambit.

The writers in the "cultural" tradition in geography have shown a more than ordinary interest in comparative evaluation of the uses of environments. Their focus has particularly fallen on the movements of ideas through conquest, contact, and migration as an influence on changing landscapes. Cultural geographers conceive the present world as the outcome of a great historical procession of ideas that emanated from a number of attested innovative centers, and accordingly they see the major periods of history as epochs in the transformation of humanity's material surroundings. This conception has encouraged their interest in the very origins and fundamental character of man and of culture. In consequence, the cultural geographer commits himself in all his work, perhaps unwittingly, to some philosophy of man.

Adhering to this tradition, I sought in an earlier book, *The Human Use of the Earth,* to show man as "inherently a restless remaker of his own world." At the time, of course, I failed to grasp the very fateful implications of that simple-minded notion. Now I should say that the cultural propensities of mankind *in themselves* tend to bring about a kind of "dislocation" of communities of men in respect of their habitats. That, I think, is the kernel of the modern ecological dilemma. Consequently, in the present essay I have tried to survey the commonplaces of geography in order to disclose, if possible, the evidences of the role of culture in the world. Culture lives through transformation of environments and peoples, and may be comprehended best, I think, within the earthbound framework of geography.

Evidence derived from verbal statements of the people under study has traditionally served as basis for the ethnological analysis of culture. But a discipline that draws its evidence for culture from the concrete artifacts, material activities, and transformations of environment produced by man, instead of taking its material from such linguistic sources, may possess its own advantages. Internal criticism of assembled data is employed in both these studies to construct hypotheses about the cultural system. Since any people has conceptions of its own culture, it is not hard to get accounts of a culture directly from the people, but surely such accounts—as ethnologists now readily acknowledge—incorporate all the well-known treacheries of language, in whatever tongue they are expressed, and also must reflect whatever wishful thinking, ignorance, and error are conventionally enshrined in any popular belief. Although the mute remains of past activity engraved in features of environment are no doubt harder to decipher, they afford another, less equivocal domain of evidence. Geography thus exemplifies, in an exceedingly crude and primitive form, a potential "behavioral" basis for the study of culture, contrasting with the established basis which is more or less "philological" in its methods. But as this essay should indicate, I believe that communication processes and structures must become the very center of our geographical concern if this potentiality is to develop.

The conception introduced here of the role of culture in the world—activity transforming habitats, engraving memory upon them—suggests a diagnosis for the plight of mankind. I must invoke the incident, however, that has crystallized the possibility for me. Some time ago, while still intending to produce a sort of introductory digest of cultural geography, I chanced to hear a neurophysiologist describe the memory-capacity of killer whales. These spirited cetaceans command astonishing recall, primarily of auditory character. They possess in their brains, both absolutely and in proportion to their body weight, much more tissue adapted to the storage of impressions than do men. The brighter *Cetaceae* apparently remember more than we do. We, however, know more anyway. Since they have the edge on us in "brains," at least in regard to available storage units, our superior position in the world as human beings may after all not rest upon those inscrutable internal mental states and powers that persistently have vexed philosophers. I venture rather to interpret the advantage of mankind as resting in environments suffused with manmade symbolism, peerless and imperishable repertories of the past experience of all the species. Transformed environments are good alternatives to bigger brains.

Perhaps big-brained Neanderthal man "thought otherwise." His development seems to have diverged from that of the *Homo sapiens* main line, feeling out the evolutionary consequences of enlarged cerebral storage as against the artifactual expression being pioneered by his more orthodox contemporary men. But Neanderthal lost out. For almost a hundred thousand years, the size of human brains—Neanderthal apart—and thus presumably the memory-capacity, have not increased. Meanwhile, though, man's interference with his own surroundings has revolutionized the world, and the earthly storehouse of experience materialized has grown almost to bursting.

Man continues ever more to revolutionize environments, and in doing so he threatens inadvertently to ruin and annihilate them. At some point, the use of all the world of nature as a raw material for mnemonic and commemorative objects has to reach its limits, as at some time the preserved results of human procreation must accumulate to overload a given habitat. If all or much of mankind goes on trying to externalize experience in environment on the present scales, the outcome is predictable. The larger collectivities of mankind, efficiently and purposefully making over things, will at last exact their final grotesque triumph over nature.

Those larger collectivities, thank God, contain their saving weakness. Who can love them, who will care enough? As means increase our motives vanish. While the systems of order and power in technological society grow ever vaster, the creative impulse in the transformation of the world becomes bureaucratized, impersonal, and ultimately meaningless. Efficiency may increase—for a while—as the inverse of untidy personal involvement. But the memory that men externalize is personal; its dominating content even now is personal identity; our handiwork betokens timeless selfhood. I should argue that the hopes and destinies that drive mankind will not submit for long to perfect rational coordination, and that the urge to transform the environment can only flourish when the individual's autonomy is paramount. Anomie, disaffection, frivolity, and boredom signal a rebellion in industrial societies that may largely thwart the further massive violation of environments. Defiance of *the system* has itself become a vehicle of creativity, and personal direct encounter with the world of "nature," an emerging value. Man may henceforth seek increasingly to find, in modest individual domains devoid of cosmic threat, the scope for personal expression and commemoration. The creative or expressive urge may thus emerge in sublimated, or rather perhaps in restored and more authentic form, before catastrophe occurs. For the very means of massive transformation of the world, aside from threatening a cataclysm, almost surely rob that very transformation of its human motive and fulfillment.

In such circumstances, when even people who command such powerful technologies can hardly understand the "reasons" or the "motives" for their fateful acts and choices, the sources and controls of what men take as right and reasonable must become of vital interest. The study of culture is not then merely an esoteric pastime; it is central to the comprehension of man's gravest problems. But a catalog of customs or of attitudes will not suffice. I think the *life* of culture as transferral of experience is the vital thing.

The present essay treats of the flow of culture, that is, of communication among men and, in a broader sense, among all the separate elements we may discern within the earth-continuum, wherever man is implicated. Communication manifested in environments is considered as crucial to man's role and fate. This crude and incomplete transactional account at least may indicate the possibility of learning something of the earthly dialectic that entails man's destiny.

Someone has said that knowledge proceeds by alternating stages of overcomplication and oversimplification. Grand principles are periodically enunciated, then gradually encumbered with amendments as familiarity with the data grows, until at last the edifice collapses and a new grand principle is promulgated. I have no true grand principles to offer here, but probably am oversimplifying. Whoever reads this book with patience will perceive that it was produced in a state of "unclear certainty": it asserts that something big is there, but cannot show it very clearly. The full disclosure of the cultural process will require much more geography.

Accordingly, this essay offers neither an exegesis nor a model. No attempt has been made to justify statements on the basis of earlier geographic literature, although the perspicacious reader will encounter much familiar matter. A formal argument from written precedent requires another book. In consequence of this point, the footnote lover will be cruelly disappointed, for I thought it best totally to cast aside what might have been misleading trappings of authority. The data are not all that recondite. I should like to acknowledge precedent and proprietorship of any ideas I may have kidnapped unwittingly from other writers; but since the essay was so naively and innocently conceived that the actual paternity of its ideas was not recorded, I can only do justice to any previous authors of my thoughts by thanking here, in blanket fashion as it were, all and any who detect something of their own likeness in it.

A model purporting to account for outcomes of communication processes upon the scale envisioned here would be presumptuous, if not preposterous, at this time. I make no apology for not explaining either exactly how things happen, or how to predict exact results of what I claim is happening. Plenty of good work is going on already upon such topics as culture history, perception, and diffusion, and I am satisfied to offer some critical perspective on such work.

The reader not familiar with the geographic background may consult companion volumes in the series, *Foundations of Cultural Geography,* listed on the cover of this volume. This essay was initially conceived as an introduction and overview of that series, and it still remains congruent with the other volumes. Not every fact, of course, will correspond to something in another volume, but some orientation in particular topics as well as their bibliography will thereby be assured. To be sure, I know of nothing adequate in English except some chapters in linguistics texts on aspects of the geography of languages discussed herein; but luckily the data themselves are easily obtained and the reasoning is not very technical. A good atlas and a sound encyclopedia will suffice to document and clarify the detailed information used.

The stimulation of working with fellow contributors to the *Foundations of Cultural Geography* has been important in encouraging this essay, as have also welcome influences from colleagues and from students, particularly at Simon Fraser University but also at Texas (Austin) and during visits elsewhere. I hope the result is no great discredit to those influences.

PHILIP L. WAGNER

West Vancouver
June 1971

Contents

Environments
and
Peoples

CHAPTER 1

universals
of cultural geography

The world is a kind of discourse among men. Their handiwork communicates, and societies are conversations. We see the rich, diverse geography of man-made landscapes as resulting from the operations of communication processes that in themselves are rather uniform and simple.

Cultural variety, with its countless geographical expressions, possesses intrinsic interest and aesthetic appeal. One of the real pleasures of geography lies in the appreciation of this variety, for it offers some of the most substantial rewards of traveling. The surprise and delight evoked by the world's diversity are a worthy end in themselves.

More grave and practical concern, as well, attaches to the cultural aspects of geography. Cultural dispositions inevitably influence technical or economic undertakings and color all international relationships. Economic development, for example, is essentially an alteration of the so-called cultural landscape, and it works through culture change. Local concepts and local customs are important everywhere in practical affairs.

Geographic knowledge also educates. Just as the adage that "travel is broadening" rings true, an informed and tolerant awareness of human differences and potentialities seems expected in the educated person. The fate and ways of others have long helped illuminate our own. A comparative outlook, if not a fully relativistic one, inheres in modern Western thinking. The study of geography in particular has, ever since the Age of Discovery, formed an essential part of European cultures and their offshoots, and afforded impetus to humanistic and scientific thought.

The many geographical relationships between environments and peoples exemplified around the world invite examination, more especially, for the light they cast upon the place of the individual human being in the world, in both the concrete and the more abstract sense. Despite the differences of geography, and regardless of the placement of their cultures on some technological scale, all men share in a common nature and a common fate, and their deeper relationships with environments are fundamentally alike. It is these universal and consistent aspects of cultural geography, not the colorful diversity, or the politically or economically opportune particulars, that here concern us.

The geographical forms—concrete visible features of landscape, as well as the more elusive spatial structures—that human life creates conform to certain basic regularities wherever they are found. The manner in which languages, for instance, become areally distributed and differentiated probably varies only slightly from one culture to the next. The growth and spread of a religion, anywhere and anytime, again follows just one fundamental pattern. Universal geographical properties can likewise be discerned in such other earthly aspects of mankind's life as settlements, technology, economies, the state, and the constitution of societies. Herein they are consulted for their lessons.

Human Behavior and the Environment

Obviously, systematic regularities of individual human behavior have to be not only inherent in, but crucial to, these larger geographic manifestations. Otherwise, the patterns would appear only fortuitously and inconsistently. A rational description of individual human behavior, however, to say nothing of its prediction, still seems chimerical today. The argument must rest, accordingly, on arbitrary premises, and whatever inferences follow will remain contingent on these premises' validity.

The familiar and legitimate conception of life as a creative process inspires the heuristic invention of the figure of Expressive Man. He reveals himself to his fellows in his actions and commemorates himself before succeeding ages through enduring material creations. He regards the world as the instrument of his insistent selfhood and mankind as his audience. All society is a "mutual admiration society," as men perpetually exchange the tokens of their own vitality and identity. Let this image be the core of our cultural geography.

All men enter early into, and remain enmeshed in, ceaseless sensory contact and interchange with their fellows. People thus involved react to, and mutually influence, each other. In a given social-sensory milieu, a particular performance tends to elicit consistent responses from an individual's companions, just as he tends to assume an identifiable role. People, notoriously, do not watch uncomprehendingly and impassively what their neighbors do; nor, in the presence of others, will they act mindlessly and meaninglessly. The imputation to human acts of sig-

2

nificance, deliberately and intelligibly conveyed to those familiar with the actor's repertory, we take for granted.

People who are socially related can communicate. What they do communicate, however, may in its particulars elude a stranger. It can nevertheless fairly be supposed that identity and vitality, however expressed according to the culture and the social context, invariably constitute the crux of what communication imparts at its deepest level. Selfhood experienced and manifested through action in the world must, indeed, count as a chief distinguishing attribute of mankind.

The artificial world of man is made of monuments. It hardly strains the imagination to conceive the birth of true mankind as having taken place at some time fifty thousand to a hundred thousand years ago, when glorious cave art, decorated burials, rich ornament of weapons, and mighty deeds of prowess like giant mammal hunts and perilous migrations attest a new level of pride and style that must have been self-conscious. Is it not plausible to say that man created himself as man when he discovered his selfhood? And perhaps he did so while brooding for the first time on his own mortality.

The expression of a human self, more explicit than the ordinary animal's signal of its presence, manifests a temporal dimension. Selfhood pierces through a moment and extends deep into a past and onward into a future. It cannot be fully environed, as an animal existence can, nor encompassed in the working of some instantaneous mechanism. This fact conditions all of cultural geography.

The meaning of environment for cultural geography goes much deeper than the immediate spatial surroundings, or the field of sensory perceptions, or the mere domain of mechanical contact and interaction of individual bodies, or even the habitual spatial range of individual movements. Environment has larger relevance as a momentary coexistence among varied presences, human and artifactual. Through it a person may experience vicarious exposure to people, things, and places that are distant or remote in time. Environment at any instant is participation in a multitude of histories. Its chains of personal acquaintance afford direct connection to all ancestral and contemporary mankind. In the substance and the style of artifacts, it immobilizes and immortalizes lives and acts now gone. Through it, too, the individual, creating, may embark into a future that transcends his limitation of mortality.

This enormous weight of representation, or symbolism, that suffuses all environments is inherent within the temporal dimension. The expression of the self through action has not only temporal directions, but also a formative effect upon the self, fixing the imprint of particular environments and what they symbolize. Whether intentional or accidental, artificial or spontaneous in nature, the features of environments are liable to stand for something and refer through time and distance to potentialities of experience. Accordingly, that reaction to environment which we call perception consists of far more than mere tropisms. In effect, any given

3

environment of the moment is of a piece with the unbroken fabric of a life, and through it run the warp-and-woof strands of the perceiver's continuous existence and experience. A man's perceptions, therefore, are his very private property. Some intimation of their nature comes, however, out of our thoroughly selective and repetitive usage of conventional symbolisms. Much-reiterated associations disclosed in material forms attest to habits of perception. Symbols, deliberately marshaled and manipulated, serve the express end of conditioning perception. Perception itself exists as part of a larger universe of communication, as response to actual or inferred expression. Its characteristic functions, interpretation and evaluation, are uses of symbolism. Perception searches for conventional, and therefore communicable, expression. The capacity for this expression is the gift of a society.

Culture and Communication

Several persons who experience the same environment should be similar. Children of a single home tend to resemble one another. Sedentary villagers draw much in common from their surroundings. But experience of nearly identical material environments can produce two altogether different kinds of person when the social positions are not alike. Any environment a person occupies has social aspects. Ordinarily, the attentiveness of human beings toward their fellows insures involvement with (and also sharp discriminations among) the latter. Society, partaking of temporality and bringing together selves in action and reaction, contributes to environment's net impact a selective and directive influence on individuals. Exerted socially within environments, applied through symbolism, this selective and directive influence imparts culture.

Culture represents man's uniqueness and creativity in the world. The so-called cultural features of the map depict human works. Systematic variations among customs and beliefs from area to area are also commonly ascribed to "cultures." Culture is hence a universal human property, appearing in many different guises. Frequently, too, "culture" signifies the reputedly highest aspirations and disciplines of man—the arts, philosophies, devotions, and manners that are held to dignify and liberate. Such "culture" embodies the noblest forms of any of the numerous distinct human "cultures."

The foregoing notions of culture relate to social and environmental processes. Culture consists of systematically communicated experience—what men learn and can teach, or what is learned and taught in a human society and graven into its material surroundings. But perhaps a rigorous definition of "culture" serves less purpose than does a clear idea of how to use the notion. Let culture consist in how men think, with its consequences. The evidence of culture, by this view, must lie in human behavior and in artifacts. Internal consistencies, within what human beings do and say and make, reveal their culture's pattern. Form, arrangement, distribution, and like attributes, whether pertaining to assemblages of words, objects, or motions, make up a partial sample of a culture, and numerous such samples taken together may document the culture's constituting principles. All behavior and its products, considered as symbolic, should communicate something of the conventions that make up the given culture. Whatever mental states occur in cultures thus can be apprehended, like perception, only when coaxed into assuming a sensible shape. Along with verbal formulas, ritual performances, art motifs, and all other such ethnographic evidence, the geographic dispositions of a society in themselves also help in this way to manifest the culture.

The interest herein, however, does not lie primarily in cataloging such intentional symbolisms, fascinating and important though they may be. Their particularity and diversity frustrate the intentions of the best compilers. Geographers can do justice to the cultural, symbolic content of a landscape only after slow and sympathetic study of its idiosyncrasies and subtleties. As individuals are always exceptional, so places in this respect are always unique.

But the principles of symbolism *per se* and the principles of any one symbolic system differ altogether, and the concrete contents of any single communication belong to an order different from the ubiquitous features and structures of all communication systems. In this study, the geographic sources of culture, rather than its substance, come to the forefront. Cultural geography becomes, by this construction, a study of the process of location of cultural elements and systems. This particular model or myth uses communication to account for cultural location; and behavior, artifacts, and landscapes are just clues to the operations of communication. Communication, the explanatory principle, when necessary can stretch enough, conceptually, to include all possible behavior, artifacts, and man-induced environmental states, which all register patterns learned in social intercourse. In fact, it becomes difficult to separate the communication process from the substance of culture if one takes the view propounded here, that all behavior, in a social-sensory context, *is* communication. Then artifacts and acts function first of all as symbols, and the landscape is a kind of theater possessing many stages. A man learns his cues, memorizes his lines, and interprets his roles. This imagery of drama comes much closer to the "model" than do cold technologies of code and channel.

The subsequent discussion focuses first upon the general processes of cultural distribution and differentiation in terrestrial space, as well exemplified by language; then upon more highly structured systems, of which religion furnishes an excellent case; next on the total environment as a synergetic communications medium, illustrated in patterns of settlement; and then successively upon individual learning and teaching in technology, inter-areal communication under the forms of economies and

5

states as comprehensive communication systems, and education in the social system as matrix of individual life and expression. The general worldwide panorama that emerges establishes a broad base for rational assessment of certain wider problems in the geography and history of culture. The topics cited form, together, instruments for universal reasoning about all cultures, as well as for grasping some of their distinguishing particularities.

Geography is how you use it. Herein we explore the subject to discover where man is in life as well as in the world. We map the central places of awareness and emotion. The search for generality leads toward rediscovery of individuality. Environment as facet and condition of our selfhood, the "geographic grid" of living, is beheld as giving outlines to peoples, and bearings to the individual procession through existence. Necessarily, this exploration is imaginary. Like any commentary on existence, it is only speculative and interpretive. It charts a vital void, but not, one trusts, without respecting what is soundly known already, for there is whence it must embark.

CHAPTER 2 *processes of distribution and differentiation*

The geographical growth of a culture proceeds more or less like other kinds of growth. Of course, not the culture in the strictest sense but rather the community imbued with it can grow and differentiate in space. A culture as an incorporeal reality may well expand its scope, acquiring new particulars and even new dimensions, but not new territory. So a people, bearers of a culture, spread it when they spread their settlements. Conversely, their territories may diminish, or they may defect to other cultures, so the area belonging to the culture shrinks or even disappears.

Growth, however, connotes not merely an increase in size or area, but equally a gradual differentiation in the growing body. In this regard as well, a culture shows its similarity to other entities. Even as its area, or rather that of its bearers, expands, it will ordinarily undergo progressive breakdown into local variants. Unlike an organism, though, a cultural community in growth need not develop into a closely articulated, interacting system of differentiated parts. A better model of its differentiation is the family, with each new generation in its turn departing and, as descendants multiply, the earlier resemblance and connection among the members weakening. In varying degree the growth and differentiation of a cultural community show parallels with those of families; in each case outside influences penetrate and change the system, and new environments exert selective effects on emerging forms.

As it differentiates, a culture receives both extrinsic contributions and external selective influences from the environment; yet purer situations do exist in which certain phases of cultural growth and differentiation take place almost autonomously, with virtually no perturbations. The

7

geographical dynamics of languages afford a striking instance of territorial processes of this kind.

Lessons from Latin

The geography of a language is the geography of its users, once again. Like most of geography, it resists comprehension unless presented in a temporal dimension; its spatial patterns express a momentary state in moving processes. Its figures are directional. The grand principle of this geography of language consists of a subsisting opposition between centripetal and centrifugal forces. In linguistic terms, it is a perpetual war between standard and nonstandard usages. But the usages or forms concerned, pervading the speech of given members of a population, possess a concrete spatial distribution.

Let an example seek to clarify the principle. The language of the Romans, over the span of their millennium, steadily expanded its domain. Within that time, of course, the language changed substantially, so that the Latins who lived squeezed in among the Umbrians, Volscians, Etruscans, and other local peoples in the earliest days of Rome spoke something very different from the highly polished language of Imperial times. In any case, the Romans spread their language as their sway extended. Merchants, settlers, soldiers, and administrators took up residence in conquered areas of Italy, the Iberian Peninsula, Gaul, the Balkans, and Africa, and the inhabitants therein acquired for themselves the language of their new masters. By the early centuries of the Christian era, Latin not only had come to be employed habitually by the populations of an area embracing almost all of Europe south and west of the Rhine and the Danube—and by some beyond this line—but had acquired a refined standard form, enshrined in a splendid literature.

The Roman soldiers and assimilated local tribes, we may imagine, used a notably less elegant or literary Latin. Indeed, from zone to zone within the Empire, usage must always have varied, given the very dissimilar native tongues which Latin overlay, and also given differences in the sources of the mixed "Roman" military and civilian migration to the provinces. So the uniformity of the notoriously nonstandard Latin of the provinces was something less than complete even at the start. Nonetheless, substantially a single language area filled all of southwest Europe. Only Greek, not long earlier established firmly by conquest and trade around the eastern Mediterranean, withstood replacement.

Latin remained, effectively, the standard language of the western part of the Empire for two thousand years, even long after it had ceased to be spoken in recognizable form among the ordinary people. Writers, orators, and emperors, and later, scribes and monks labored to maintain and defend its standard forms, and it continued as the common language of the learned of a continent. Up through the nineteenth century, not only the Catholic Church but European universities kept Latin alive; it served as the language of scholarly dissertations and addresses and was a badge of the educated man. Only lately has its primacy even in liturgy been modified.

Yet Latin, despite those centralizing influences, commenced to differentiate as soon as it reached new soil. No sooner did the military set up camp than they began using newly invented expressions. In a few generations, every one of the Roman provinces undoubtedly possessed its own special pronunciations, idioms, and slang. Given a thousand years to ripen in certain places, the little differences turned into a myriad of local dialects. Similarities among dialects decreased with distance, and dialects far removed in space differed greatly. Within the medieval welter of Romance dialects—as the lineal descendants of spoken Latin came to be known—a few more or less standard usages began to crystallize around certain courts and merchant cities, or in literary traditions like those of the Provençal and Catalan troubadours. Meanwhile, the standard Latin of the Church and the universities still prevailed in its own sphere. Whereas the variations among dialects were gradual, and they seldom gave rise to clear-cut boundaries, the standard languages like Castilian, French, and Provençal (or rather the politically prescribed domains of their use) met along sharp frontier lines. Topographic barriers in some places did sharply divide zones. Isolated in the Balkans, for example, lived a host of Proto-Romanian dialects, extending from Istria to Moldavia and to the Peloponnesus. The eastern coast and islands of the Adriatic harbored another (now extinct) set of Romance dialects. Sardinia had its own aberrant dialect family, as did particularly isolated Alpine valleys.

The geography of Romance languages today exists on the two distinct levels of standard languages proper and of dialects, the two contrasting keenly. Furthermore, new phases in the differentiation of the daughter dialects of Latin now transpire in the Americas, as French turns into Haitian creole and Quebec patois, and Portuguese and Spanish diversify region by region.

Although the Arab-Moorish invasion and occupation partially truncated the dialect development of Romance languages in Spain and Portugal, with further disturbances following the Reconquest, and despite a nearly complete eradication of the dialects of France through deliberate policy, most areas remain diversified in dialect to this day. The "Italian" of home use in rural Sicily is absolutely unintelligible to a Piedmontese. Even in France, where the standard usages largely triumphed, regional contrasts reassert themselves.

To recapitulate the process that Latin and its offshoots exemplify:

1. the initial spread of a relatively uniform linguistic usage; followed by
2. immediate onset of processes of local diversification; partially off-set by
3. explicit efforts at standardization, resulting ultimately in

9

4. complete divorce of the artificially preserved standard language from the new descendant vernaculars; so that
5. (a) the former standard eventually becomes a "dead" language, having no true native speakers but perhaps still ritually employed; and
   (b) new standards arise out of the living vernaculars, and new attempts to standardize the speech over larger areas commence, leading in time, probably, to a repetition of the same history.

Ideally, the geography of any language that develops unimpeded should feature a mosaic of local dialects, varying continuously by small degrees with distance in each direction, upon which a standard language may or may not be superimposed and used concurrently. The magnitude of variation among dialects over a given distance ought hypothetically, in such cases, to correspond neatly to the age of the whole system.

A nearly constant overall rate of linguistic change through time does appear to hold in general, at least if measured by retention of certain crucial vocabulary items. Empirical investigation shows approximately 80 percent of so-called "basic" word stock remaining recognizably alike between related languages and dialects after one thousand years of separation. But this is a purely temporal matter. Unfortunately, no one seems to have attempted measurement of the corresponding distance-decay function in space, which, if feasible despite its obvious pitfalls, should prove interesting.

Development of Standard Languages

In most linguistic evolution, accidents of proximity and frequent intercourse have operated to induce some degree of standardization. A language community in most cases, however, probably lacks any expressly centralizing forces. Differentiation may sometimes proceed totally unhindered, and conceivably effect within a given lapse of time a more pronounced dissimilarity among the dialects than might occur if standardizing influences existed. The cases of widely spoken languages, connected with enduring national political systems and buttressed by literacy, stand out as exceptional.

Normal situations would more resemble that of prehistoric Indo-European, ancestor of all the speech of Europe, the upper Middle East, and the northern portion of the Indian subcontinent. As reconstructed, the history of this ancient stock involves an outward surge from a center somewhere north of the Black Sea around 2000 B.C., and a long and complicated series of migrations, conquests, and countermarches, culminating in the present immense extension of the daughter languages. If the parent Indo-European language ever had a single standard form, it must have diversified the moment the tribes that spoke it set forth on their wanderings. Some scholars account for the striking parity of development in so many Indo-European language divisions, however, by postulating a closely united conqueror elite, few in numbers, who (according to their version) circulated widely and maintained close liaison, imposing for centuries their language in almost unvarying form on numerous and widespread subject peoples.

Unwritten myths and legends, rote sayings, and ritual formulas may well have served for a while almost like a literary tradition to perpetuate accepted forms. But although such conservative repositories of linguistic pattern apparently do inhibit change somewhat—illiterate bards can repeat archaic stanzas flawlessly—any ostensibly fixed oral tradition must slowly evolve, albeit much less rapidly than spontaneous colloquial speech. Indo-European, accordingly, has undergone such change within the last few thousand years that only experts recognize the unity of its descendants.

Sometimes a canonical literary language, invested in sacred texts and guarded and propagated by a priesthood or bureaucracy of scribes, as in the case of Latin, Sanskrit, Mandarin, and Arabic, provides a vehicle for elite discourse. Yet vernaculars and dialects irresistibly diverge from it. Attempts to bring the living popular language under the control of long established standard forms prove futile. So even a written and thus immutable model cannot halt the drift. As the instances of Latin, Greek, and Shakespeare's English show, even the phonetic readings of the changeless written texts will alter with the times and fashions.

Widespread or even heavily preponderant use of standard languages throughout national territories constitutes a striking and relatively unusual feature displayed by the cultural geography of Europe and its offshoot areas. Virtually everyone in France, Great Britain, and Sweden, for instance, makes exclusive use of standard French, English, or Swedish (with occasional exceptions). This represents the fruit of long, persistent efforts of the central regimes and cultural elites of these countries, as the French case demonstrates.

The growth of the French state centered around the Île-de-France, beginning with the institution of the Frankish states in the late first millennium A.D. In the year 842, the Strasbourg Oath acknowledged the prevalence of Romance languages in the western realm of Charlemagne's old domains. The Paris court, as its influence increased, promoted the use of its local dialect but had to contend with the rival southern *langue d'oc* employed and embellished by the medieval troubadours, as well as with whatever usages were current in then-independent or insurgent Romance areas like sometime-English Aquitaine, half-Celtic Brittany, the Norman settlements on the Channel, and Burgundy. Consolidation of political power around Paris under the Bourbon kings increasingly imposed the French of Île-de-France. Probably the seventeenth century was decisive, for then a host of dramatists, essayists, and poets wrote in the new standard forms, and simultaneously the monarch's military adventures mixed men from all the realm and taught them the king's French. The

Académie Française, peerless watchdog of the chastity of the language, was founded then (circa 1635). Engineers built roads and bridges unparalleled for that time in Europe, stimulating internal trade and travel, with their homogenizing tendencies. The courts and *parlements* began to insist on "correct" language for their proceedings. The Revolution ushered in further efforts in the same direction, with the abolition of the old provincial privileges, the institution of a national school system, massive military activity, encouragement of arts and sciences, and rapid growth of literacy.

Concurrently with all these processes, the dialects of France themselves remained in evolution, but through steady attrition and parcellation they must have become increasingly debilitated and corrupted. Relegated to a place of disdain and ridicule, a dialect would become a social liability to be eschewed by all who could acquire the prestige of standard language. Thus standardization gradually advanced in consequence of deliberate public policies, as well as under influence of informal social pressures. By the late nineteenth century, few Frenchmen habitually spoke dialects. In rustic settings, Breton, Basque, Catalan, Provençal, Piedmontese, Flemish, and especially the German dialects of Alsace and Lorraine maintained themselves precariously; Corsica remained Italian-speaking. French preponderated in the cities everywhere except in Alsace, severed from France after 1870. A certain disdain toward anything but literary French, today still characteristic of educated Frenchmen, embarrassed deviant speakers. Nonetheless—a crucial point—colloquial forms based on the standard language mushroomed in every social class, trade, and neighborhood. In familiar settings, variants developed that soon digressed considerably from the common language, so much so that the distinctive *argots* of different social groups and urban neighborhoods, studded with their own odd words and turns of phrase, are often unintelligible to strangers. Regional vocabularies and, even more, differences in pronunciation also tended to persist enough to signal geographical origins of speakers.

The case in Britain differed somewhat, since to the influence of standardizing poets of the English or the Scots traditions, and to the result of intercourse in fleet and court and market, strong class distinctions added their effects. The major speech disparities, more geographical in France, are more social (and perhaps wider) in Great Britain. In England, as in other countries like Poland, Sweden, Hungary, and Russia, a central zone of contact, geographically and linguistically more or less intermediate among competing dialects, gave rise to the emerging standard speech, blending forms from all sides and representing a kind of average pattern. In certain cases, political and religious circumstances fostered, not one unifying standard, but two or more rival standards within an area of related dialects. Thus Flemish, as one official language of the Belgian nation after 1830, differentiates itself in some very minor ways from the neighboring Dutch, and both Dutch and Flemish stand deliberately apart from the related German, although their dialects do merge along the borders. Scots vocabulary and pronunciation claim equal dignity with the "received" English standard. More flagrant competition sets off Slovak, developed under strong Hungarian impact, from its near relative, the Czech of German-influenced Bohemia and Moravia. Ukrainian boasts a standard form in part because its speakers, once subjects of the Polish kingdom, adhered to Uniate Catholicism, unlike their Muscovite-ruled relatives. Two written standards, in different alphabets, exist for Serbo-Croatian, according primarily with religious differences, and cutting right across the major dialect division proper. In Norwegian, a new standard built on country speech has gradually taken over from a basically Danish court language, and in Greek two patterns, one based on modern popular usage and the other echoing ancient classical forms, compete. Almost every other European language would exhibit similar complexities. Most languages elsewhere in the world today, except those of European derivation, cannot claim any standard form, although the progress of literacy does favor agreement on some one pattern, at least for printed communication.

Language standardization involves political activity in most instances, as these cases intimate. The relevant aspect here, however, is their imposition by a geographically central and, ordinarily, socially dominant agency upon surrounding domains, and the counterforce of local improvisation and diversification that affects them. The vicissitudes of English abroad illustrate the drifting apart of both popular vernaculars and literary standards in the absence of complete political and communications unity. Even the Commonwealth countries speak an English of their own, and each a different one. The origins of North American English dialects go back to Britain, but these dialects also reflect subsequent local influences within the Colonies, then the Dominion and the Republic, that shaped standards different from the British. Both dialect development and propagation of the standard language in the United States and Canada deserve more study.

A consideration of the non-European areas of Asia and Africa immediately suggests that standard languages can flourish only in a highly integrated, relatively mobilized and centralized society. There are no "French-speaking African countries," in spite of what the newspapers say, and the most nearly "English-speaking nation" of Black Africa contains at most a small elite minority of English speakers. The only African countries where any single tongue prevails are Arabic-speaking. The multiplicity of different linguistic groups combined in a typical African or Asian country (excepting the Far East) presents other geographical problems for later consideration, but in the present context it should illustrate the comparative oddity of the European linguistic situation, stemming from a special kind of nationhood.

Language and the Social Spectrum

Standardization of language presents one special instance of a much more general situation—social dialect differentiation—carried to extremes. Every distinct social group in an area is likely to speak differently. Schoolyard usage contradicts the teacher's. Hip language baffles "straights." Those who can impose their rules on language, though, are not necessarily the rich and politically powerful. English professors intimidate the *parvenus* and Presidents. Social stratification of speech extends beyond the "horizontal" dimensions of geography to "vertical" ones within society. Its geographical importance rests generally upon the fact that it attests communication patterns, that is, connections among groups and persons, which more often than not well merit geographical investigation. Obviously, we ought to query whether thieves' jargons are consistently alike from city to city, or expressions used by adolescents throughout North America obey a single set of norms. A good examination of linguistic questions like these might expose the whole skeleton of a social system.

The plight of immigrant communities in America, continuing to use the old languages in new contexts, shows how ruptures with their formerly attendant communication patterns may perceptibly alter the language. When the grandchildren of Japanese immigrants visit Japan, their pride in knowing Japanese is chastened by the islanders' reaction to omission of the honorific forms, which have been eroded away in usage in the United States or Canada. The Texas-born Spanish speaker traveling in Mexico risks derision for his "Texmex" dialect reflecting English influence and different social customs. Many children and grandchildren of immigrants perpetuate the language of the "old country" in peasant forms of half or three-quarters of a century ago, already extinct at home, and their grammar and diction, unconsciously those of the remote village, may shock and appall the European speaker of the language. Such linguistic irregularities express a geographical anomaly, a dissonance between the older pattern and the new environment, which lacks the requisite communication links. As connections atrophy the usages become devitalized.

A similar condition appears in a case like that of Scottish Gaelic, wherein a language, the body of its speakers fragmented and infiltrated with aliens, lies expiring in its home domain. Divergences increase through lack of intercourse among communities of Gaelic speakers; internally, English influence augments; and sons and daughters sheepishly conceal or cast away their declassed language heritage. If literacy prevails, its vehicle is English. In the Scottish instance, new environmental conditions, commencing with the dreadful Highland Clearances and proceeding through the period of industrialization, have engulfed the Gaelic areas bit by bit, until at last the tourist sojourners accomplish what the greedy lairds and stern mill operators could not, and their English supplants the Gaelic even in the distant isles.

Standardization always presupposes, to some extent, the acceptance by the dialect speakers of a new language, even when this standard is related closely to their mother speech. In the frequent cases where the existing dialects, of most varied origins and affinities, occur thoroughly scrambled on the map, the selection and propagation of some one of them, or of an outside candidate, in appropriately improved condition, entails formidable controversies. Again, the matter savors strongly of political problems. Regimes like those of Ethiopia and India, attempting to elevate one native language—almost invariably a minority language— into the commanding role, encounter fervent opposition from various ethnic particularists. At least in these cases a long literary tradition helps legitimize the Amharic or Hindi chosen as the common vehicle. In a great many countries without any one predominant dialect, or even any single language family in the majority, the situation is more difficult still, and an altogether alien European language may have to serve in schools, courts, and administration. But the choice of such a medium as French or English in Africa, or Russian in Soviet Central Asia, cannot fail to inflame the opponents of colonialism. Only a completely new language of some kind might satisfy all, but it will inevitably suffer from the lack of a literature and tradition of its own, and everyone will have to learn it. The adoption of Hebrew by Israel, resting on a rich tradition, was exceptional; Indonesia's successful adoption of a compromise synthesis of various Malayan languages, too, exploited the fortunate common basis of almost all the country's numerous dialects.

A standard language might best develop on the basis of a *lingua franca,* a widely spoken dialect used in trade and other transactions among different linguistic groups over a considerable area. The European languages play this role in Africa and parts of Asia, as does Arabic. Some such languages of fairly local scope available in various countries may develop into standards. Otherwise, when no single common language prevails, people often tend to acquire proficiency in several. Some degree of bilingualism or polylingualism may actually be a commoner feature, geographically, than monolingualism. The mechanisms and geographic structures of communication can clearly transcend such barriers as linguistic difference; how they do so constitutes a question of considerable importance for cultural geography.

A common device for bridging gaps of language is translation. In remote Indian villages of Middle and South America, or in settlements of Southeast Asian hill tribes, only a few elders, perhaps, will be fully conversant with the national language. Most adult males may command some rudiments of Spanish, Burmese, or whatever is the dominant administrative tongue, but the women ordinarily will lack any knowledge of it. The few fluent national-language speakers serve as interpreters on the infrequent occasions of need. A close parallel obtains in "advanced" countries whose citizens, knowing nothing of foreign languages, rely on occasional interpreters or translators. Geographical or sociological isolation explains both cases. In markets and other common meeting places for diverse groups, full or partial bilingualism may suffice in order to assure communication. Even people using two different languages, if the latter happen to resemble each other fairly closely, may converse; this occurs in the trading encounters among Indian groups in parts of Mexico, using, for example, Tzeltal and Tsotsil dialects, and again in West Africa among speakers of related Twi languages. No doubt a halting but hearty dialogue of this sort often does the job required. The bilingualism already mentioned probably occurs so widely, however, as to constitute a normal device for intergroup communication, in which neighbor peoples know each other's languages as a matter of course. Employment of a more widespread lingua franca represents a special case of bi- or polylingualism in which the speaker has mastered ordinarily not his neighbors', but some distant people's speech, and his interlocutors have done likewise. Something similar to a lingua franca can grow up crazily and crudely out of the most improbable matings of linguistic materials, in particular when traders meet native peoples. The resultant trade jargons, usually backed by no written tradition, go far afield but may not last long. So the history of European trade has left behind a host of ephemeral jargons like Chinook in northwest America, and Pidgins in the Orient, Western Pacific, and West Africa, constructed on the spot, as it were, for regional use. A lingua franca proper, which is simply an established language in widened use, like Urdu or Swahili, lasts better and preserves a greater respectability. The extreme case of a lingua franca, of course, is nothing less than a universal language.

For certain parts of the world a language map remains almost entirely hypothetical, in the absence of data; those very areas, in all likelihood, would be the ones where true bilingualism is commonest—out-of-the-way places where numerous small tribes exist, away from European influence. But even well-studied areas present problems. When dialects exist alongside a related standard language, and a person tends to fit his usage to the social situation, sometimes leaning toward the dialect and sometimes toward the literary standard, as frequently occurs in Germany, Switzerland, or Italy, for example, at what point do we declare the speaker "bilingual"? The answer can only reasonably be: When his command of two linguistic systems uniquely enables him to communicate with two distinct communities or groups.

Consider a concrete case of both bilingualism and mother tongue. The linguistic map of the state of Texas shows heavy bilingualism, reaching up to something over 50 percent along the southwestern Rio Grande Valley margin, where Spanish vies with English for dominance. People who habitually speak English at home frequently know Spanish, too; a good majority of the Spanish speakers also command some English. English-Spanish bilingualism grades off northeastward, until along the Brazos, midway across the state, it sinks to a few percent, and becomes comparable with bilingualism in other language pairs (Czech-English, German-English, a little French-English in the far southeastern corner).

Upon the map of Texas, home language shows almost the same areal pattern, although percentages differ in detail. In a city like San Antonio, however, some neighborhoods are all-Spanish, although the city as a whole is mixed.

Most of Texas belongs to that great expanse of North America over which English predominates nearly exclusively. The language map on a more comprehensive scale shows the domain of English broken only by the bloc of French in Quebec, the neighboring Maritimes, and northeastern Ontario; by a few tiny spots where native Indian languages survive; and by the ribbon of Spanish running along the southern land border of the United States, and spottily up the Rio Grande into Colorado. Such a situation typifies a modern Western country and prevails throughout a considerable part of the world. Huge territories fall to English, Russian, Spanish, and Portuguese, each with a hundred million speakers or more. The various divergent Chinese languages, possessing a unified literary standard and together, as a bloc of many hundred millions of speakers, dominating a vast area, present a special case. In contrast, throughout continental Europe, the Middle East, and South and Southeast Asia, relatively less populous language areas of middle size prevail. Several dozen languages spoken by about five million to a hundred million people occupy most of this great arc. This second pattern of linguistic realms of somewhat more modest scope contrasts, again, with a third relatively consistent one, composed of a host of small communities making up a fine mosaic that covers the bulk of Africa (south of the massive area of Arabic), the greater part of southern Asia, and portions of tropical America. Only a few languages native to these areas can account for as many as five million speakers. Thus the world language map displays three categories: true international or multinational languages, established national languages with literary and political autonomy, and local or tribal languages. Each occupies a different characteristic geographic position, and conforms to a distinct linguistic type. The strictly local languages of small area and few speakers probably exist at such a scale that social usage within the speaking community preserves a kind of standard form for them. They bear some resemblance to the local dialects of other areas, and indeed may represent nothing more than dialects. The kinds of languages—e.g., Tamil in India, Romanian in Europe, Tagalog in the Phillipines—that occur at a national level possess a single literary standard and may override a family of kindred dialects, whereas the international languages may well conform not merely to a single standard, but at least by implication to several, as do Portuguese and English. To make this map of world language communities complete, we should have to incorporate both unrelated minority languages dispersed within the large domains, like Quechua in Peru or the lesser

17

languages of Finnic origin in European Russia, for example, and the native dialects related to and spoken concurrently with the standard languages.

The map of linguistic communities just described complements the more familiar one of linguistic relationships distinguished along genetic lines. The grouping of languages by common descent discloses certain geographic circumstances governing the linguistic processes involved. The former are of two sorts: dialectic tensions between centripetal and centrifugal forces within a speech community that result in dialect formation, and migratory phenomena that shatter the neat gradient patterns that regular dialect differentiation generates.

As illustrated in the case of Latin, speech diversifies, splitting into new dialects, when it spreads over an area. Differences creep in automatically when people, separated, carry on a common heritage. Accidents, improvisations, imitations, and contaminations all play their part in setting off each independent version of the parent pattern. The less the mutual intercourse and interaction, the more divergence will occur, so difference will tend eventually to express a function of distance, time of separation, or difficulty of communication. The actual distribution of dialects does conform rather well to the model based on this assumption. However, the principle of distance decay fails to apply to dialect distribution at a certain level, roughly corresponding to the social interaction-space of a living face to face community. No one always stays right at home. The people of a locality, moving about on their ordinary business, set up connections of sufficient intensity that mutual linguistic influence overwhelms divergent tendencies, and a local near-uniformity results. A dialect, at least at the level of the single village, ordinarily constitutes an impressively unified and consistent system. Social dispositions regulate the distribution. The spatial scope of habitual intercourse defines the best dialect boundary. The barriers to sharing dialect features consist of social barriers or voids. If the general scheme of gradual variation of dialect in all directions, throughout an entire language realm, retains validity at a certain scale, it nevertheless cannot apply within the basic social areas like villages. A mosaic of such small areas, nearly uniform internally, rather than a smooth transition, best describes the typical situation.

Investigation of a number of dialect situations has revealed that intricacies of social pattern and habit extending back for centuries underlay the distributions. Patterns of parish boundaries, market areas, political jurisdictions, and military zones perpetuate themselves in dialect divisions. German dialect areas along the middle Rhine express the early modern ecclesiastical and administrative units. Some characteristics of American English cropping up repeatedly in different port cities suggest a common maritime linguistic influence. Thus, social geography and linguistic geography exhibit a good deal of connection, and the social and geographical determinants of speech type tend to coalesce. A map made of tiny mosaic bits in color might express the typical dialect situation, showing gradual color changes in all directions, shading off over the thousands of bits representing single villages. The given color continuum would have to halt abruptly somewhere, reaching a definite frontier. For in any direction, on land, migrations have eventually intervened to break off the smooth gradation. Utter unconformities indicate where major migrations have intruded, and lesser shifts reveal themselves in juxtapositions of only distantly related dialects. All the communities represented on a language map go back ultimately to successive migrations at different periods, each having settled into place amid alien neighbors or distant kin and having begun, like them, to differentiate internally in language. The familiar atlas map of languages of Europe displays the results of such a sequence of migrations.

In Europe, the blocs of Slavic, Celtic, Germanic, Romance, Uralic, and so on do not merge. Furthermore, certain divisions even within them record internal migrations of their speakers. Consider, though, how the European map depicts the successive waves of peoples, or at least of conquering elites. The Basques survive from an undated past, linguistically alone. The Celtic that moved westward and southward about 2000 B.C. across most of Europe and into Asia Minor still occurs in extreme western refuges, and shows through in countless place names elsewhere. A great surge of Romance, already detailed, overrunning Celtic in places, has retreated only from Britain, North Africa, and its German and Balkan fringes. Then Germanic, having burst into the late Roman world and left memories of briefly-ruling tribes throughout, took up its place in the heart of Europe. It waged a struggle with expanding Slavic along an eastern margin still not surely stabilized. (The independent Albanian and Greek stocks have remained in place in the south since the dawn of history, and far to the north Finnish and its Baltic neighbors entered quietly in prehistoric times and have held firm before the thrusts of Slavic and Germanic speakers.) Invaders from the steppe, advancing across Europe, left only Magyar and a few Turkic dialects to commemorate themselves, while the Arabs who infested Spain, Portugal, and the isles of the sea for centuries have left their language in Malta alone.

Europe, although linguistically a collage of fascinating complexity, has a recorded history to explain the pattern. The world linguistic map displays other histories as lavish in their scale but which are lost to memory. North America, for instance, is divided largely among the Athapascan stock in the north, Algonkian and Muskogean in the northeast and southeast respectively, Siouan-Caddoan in the center, and Uto-Aztecan in the drier west, with a welter of small groups along the western and southern peripheries. Isolates and outliers abound from Alaska down the Pacific Coast and into Middle America. Unmistakably, distributions like that of Algonkian—strung across the continent along latitude 45°N —or Hokan, rimming the valleys of California, bear witness to epics of their own. Territorial shifts and migrations continued to play a generous

19

part in the native American world right down to the European intrusion: the Plains were in turmoil because of the introduction of horses, and the plateau and desert Southwest were in the process of reapportionment, when invaded by the Europeans. The linguistic maps show the results of these histories. On other continents, similarly, language distributions intimate vast unrecovered histories of Bantu, Carib, Turk, and Malay.

But explanation of the patterns need not always rest upon the assumption of great migrations. Assimilation of resident peoples into new linguistic communities, through conquest or peaceful attraction, has surely been more instrumental than mass transplantation in altering the map of language. Certainly the city of Rome and its vicinity furnished only a minor physical contribution to the ancestry of populations later speaking Romance tongues. Europe's inhabitants, in all likelihood, today represent much less direct genetic heritage from the actual Indo-Europeans than from antecedent population stocks that took up Indo-European speech. The spread of a language like Arabic patently depended on its adoption by outsiders, as it does even now in Africa, where considerable shifts to Arabic continue in the Maghreb and Sudan. Even when migrations do happen, as from Europe to America, assimilation affecting diverse initial migrant stocks takes place.

Change of Language

Complex and unseen causes prompt a shift in language. Sometimes compulsion, at other times latent loyalties and animosities, manifestly abetted the dissemination of Arabic in the Near East and North Africa. Clearly, a change of language or acquisition of an extra one can open up desired new channels of communication and promote an individual's or a group's incorporation into an admired or envied social body. The problem of linguistic assimilation in the end relates to a family of geographic issues. It hangs on the directions, diversity, and spatial reach and social ranking of a community's communication links; upon the scale of organization in which it participates, or wishes to; upon access to resources, markets, livelihood, and other properties of certain affiliations. Thus, when the peoples of Egypt and the North African littoral turned their backs on decrepit Greek Byzantium and Latin Europe they tied themselves through the vehicle of Arabic to an Islamic world whose arts, sciences, and civil life outshone whatever they had lately known. The Chinese expansion in Asia, too, has depended at least in part upon the universal appeal of the language, giving access to a classic tradition and to important practical connections.

The influences of neighboring languages, one upon the other, mostly pertain to borrowings of vocabulary. As geographical phenomena, some particular effects, however, should be noted. In listening to various spoken languages, one may be struck by similarities of sounds and cadences among pairs of languages not close genetically but coming from adjoining areas. The phonetics of the various Indian tongues of Oregon, Washington, and British Columbia, for example, showed many uniformities despite a notable variety of origins. Tonal, monosyllabic languages of highly diverse affinities form substantial clusters in Southeast Asia, southwest Mexico, and West Africa. Language similarities may also cut across another dimension. The grammatical devices marking future-forms of verbs in several Balkan languages, for instance, also form their own anomalous spatial cluster. Again, many grammatical features are shared by Indo-European, Dravidian, and Munda languages of peninsular India. Some areal units constituted in this way have little to do with the genetics of language. The phenomenon, called "Sprachbund," apparently has dual explanations. On the one hand, what some linguists suppose to be the influence of an old common "substratum," antecedent to imposition of several new languages, perhaps may validly be cited; on the other hand, manifest communication among neighboring communities can itself promote resemblances. The peoples dwelling around Puget Sound and Georgia Strait, for instance, differed more in style of culture and in sound of speech from inland neighbors than from opposite or somewhat distant fellow boatsmen more frequently encountered.

In such cases, the problem relates to partial but not full adoption of a language, so relatively minor, indeed, that it does not disturb the major pattern. The nature of languages dictates functional unity and close internal systemic adjustment, so that casual intrusions of borrowed sounds or morphological features would only fit in sparingly. Such a stricture probably does not apply to vocabulary. Some languages, having borrowed lavishly, may in fact retain hardly more than the morphological skeleton of their old selves. Persian is substantially a combination of older Iranian, Arabic, and Turkish vocabularies in fairly even proportions. The native element in the vocabulary of Albanian occupies a minority position. Creole speech in the West Indies apparently consists of European words arranged in an African order and pronounced in obedience to African norms; according to the source of words, there are French and English and Spanish varieties of Creole.

The freedom of words to migrate suggests an independent geography for them, along with a host of histories. No educated person fails to note the presence in his language—whatever one it might be—of technical terms and ordinary roots from other sources. English has a very impressive component of Greek, another of Latin, and yet another of French, alongside its Germanic core. Japanese displays parallel vocabularies of Chinese and of native origin. The course of word migrations reaches far back into prehistory; even some prehistoric streams of influence have left clues. Many words in the classical languages of Europe have cousins in Egyptian and Semitic, all of them imputedly descending from unknown ancient Mediterranean sources. Names and other words have drifted

21

about, too, between China and Europe since early times. But the volume of word flow, like that of communication in general, has increased with the growth of connections during certain key periods, including perhaps most notably the present age of mass communications. Word distributions, in sum, are consequences and therefore clues of geographical connections.

What rationale explains the borrowing of words, and particularly the adoption of a language? Is it simply that people always try to widen their horizons, or broaden their opportunities, by adopting the language or vocabulary of widest currency? Obviously not, because in that case a universal language, logically, would rapidly emerge triumphant. On the other hand, does everyone doggedly retain his mother tongue and resist all others? Such a theory is also false. The social dimension would appear to be the crucial one; a person speaks what his social roles require and his social aspirations dictate. Mere conformity with neighbors and companions, along with integration on a normal basis into some community, prescribe adoption of the appropriate language. Being in a particular place, a man knows well enough what to speak there. Free entry into groups and territories does not necessarily follow from the mastery of their language, though. Rather, language follows upon other social qualifications and is, for the most part, subservient to them. Hence, although the growth of dialect exhibits a pattern and process subject to direct geographical analysis, the explanation of language change as a geographical phenomenon, and of the dispersals of vocabularies, demands an understanding of other social factors as well.

If linguistic change encounters social barriers and follows lines of social force, as it were, what are the prospects for acceptance of a universal language, and by implication, of a world culture? To digress a moment, consider the implications of the process of dialect differentiation. Any worldwide standard, of language or perhaps of culture, would certainly undergo the same kind of decomposition in each locality as any present language does, even though powerful technical countermeasures would apply. Diversity would spontaneously and insistently reassert itself. Furthermore, any effort to compress the social usages and language patterns into a single mold would inescapably require a highly diversified organization, assuring the operation of the mechanisms of communication that bound the world together. Different slangs and technicians' lingoes would inevitably arise, and at most a few basic rules of grammar might universally hold sway among all the multitude of particular vocabularies incidental to the very operation of the universal system.

Language in the narrow sense has illustrated this discussion. Had the data sufficed, the same principles might have been exposed in some other, complementary human communication codes. All sorts of sensory media enter into use for these. Color and rhythm of speech, facial and bodily gesture, touch, intragroup spatial arrangement—all play their part. All would have their own histories and geographies that conform to regular principles, akin at least to those governing speech. The degree of that kinship is an important question in itself.

Similarly, all the manifest declarative uses of property and performance arrest our notice. Who fails to recognize people by their dress and posture? Students and professors dress differently. And who misses the eloquence of custom? Germans keep their cars polished; Italians grow vegetables. Furthermore, such expressions vary with the mood and wish. A jaunty walk means confidence, a sloppy desk depression or confusion. Even deeper lie the marks of a person: a voice on the telephone instantly recognized, a footstep heralding a welcome visit, a scrap of handwriting evoking memories. And does not disorder in a loved one's speech or movements generate alarm?

How much, we might ask, of such "language" is truly universal, and what is peculiar to each culture? Without a doubt, some traits stand apart. Certain standards and habits become diffused like language items, and people assimilate new values and skills. Sojourners "go native" in the tropics. Neighborhoods attempt to coax or shame an errant family into tidy habits. A great deal gets communicated without benefit of speech. The codes, if clearly known, would have geographies. It develops that "culture" differs not so much from "language" as we thought.

For cultures as wholes, then, inferences from language may apply. Apportioned out among many relatively isolated localities, not only patterns of speech, but those of dress, kinship reckoning, technology in general, religion, and all else might well diversify with time. On the other hand, a central agency might well exert a standardizing influence in these respects, disseminating technical directives and spiritual guidance. This obviously happens. Furthermore, the map of cultures (in whatever guise we visualize them), like the map of language, inescapably must register migrations that have intruded to break the regularity of gradual spatial differentiation. In each of these regards, the areal necessities of communication systems decisively assert themselves. Thus far, those systems of communication have been dealt with only grossly, enough to discern general properties. Their structure takes on greater consequences in the discussion that ensues.

CHAPTER 3
structures
of dissemination

Communication flow, the lifeblood of all culture, runs in certain ramified and yet intermittently converging channels. Hence it generates a very different sort of pattern from that of the solid areas and their boundaries and subdivisions previously discussed. Comparison with the circulatory system of the body would be misleading; the networks of communication more resemble earth-surface streams of water, except that they diverge in all directions from a multitude of separate origins, and their traffic carries an inexhaustible commodity that constantly increases and reduplicates.

Gossip chains, for instance, do their bit to enliven or perhaps envenom small town and village life. Information passes orally among a usually obvious coterie, who do not scruple on occasion to embellish their reports. After the item has been broadcast over the chain, "everyone in town knows about it," often to the horror of the victim. But all sorts of other information also move over similar networks, and any villager has access to voluminous reports on a variety of topics. Family affairs, farming methods, plans for festivals, the weather, and a great many special topics have their own discussion and intelligence systems. Some agencies of information function exclusively and explicitly in that role, such as church, school, club, more or less corporate working groups, ritual societies and brotherhoods, and political organizations. Other groups of persons less formally constituted like the gossip chain, fulfill a similar role almost as faithfully. All of these institutions, formal and informal, operate conjointly to disseminate information. Such institutional connections regulate and guarantee the flow of communication, which constitutes the main business of these institutions.

A disparity always exists, in communication, between sender and receiver, the one who tells and the one who listens. The difference in roles may entail some permanent pattern of flow, so that information passes only in one direction, for example, or the flow may take place only at the initiative of one of the parties. Culture in fact represents an emerging product of information flowing out from centers of standardizing agencies, and coming up against the counterflows that go on at the local level.

A flow in only one direction and the control of communication by only one party both affect a number of different networks that impinge on the same individual or place. Multiple networks inevitably pass along contradictory information and inconsistent directives all the time, so that rivalry among various agencies cannot fail to play a major part in complicating life. Competing institutions demand a choice. The cultural field of forces seldom dictates one single, definite result. The learning process, furthermore, selects among the contents of communication to accommodate what was previously accepted in light of experienced compatibility with environment. Communication filters information to a person through a double screen of past experience and present environment.

Communication operates through organized connections—even rumors spread chiefly through established channels. The pathways of communication, each one finite and distinctive, and collectively making up a definite articulated system, do not constitute a spatially uniform medium through which impulses may move, like the molecules of a gas or the crystals of an alloy. Therefore, the term "diffusion" hardly does justice to what happens when information spreads. Highly specialized and specific structures are concerned in these cultural processes.

Christianity as Communication

Religious institutions offer an illuminating instance of the structural aspects of communication systems. The Roman Catholic Church, largest of all organized religious bodies, devotes a large portion of its enterprise to a continual process of communication. The governance and structure of the church, and to a large degree the work of its ministers and functionaries, conform to basic principles of information flow. The church's definition of itself as "apostolic" emphasizes this role in communicating the Gospel and kindred information.

Pronouncing on matters of faith or morality, the Pope, according to Catholic doctrine, speaks infallibly. No earthly voice may contradict a papal promulgation, for the Pope is considered directly subject to divine guidance in such matters. In less crucial matters, he still retains his primacy, but the bishops and even laymen exercise considerable autonomous power and initiative in church affairs. However, authority in general descends through the ramifying hierarchy, each level depending successively more upon the authority and direction of superiors. The territorial basis of the Church, beginning with division of the land into parishes and missionary fields, themselves grouped into dioceses and provinces, expresses an admirable orderliness. But numerous special congregations, patriarchates, titular bishoprics, monastic orders, vicarates, and even secular appendages express the elaborate functions vested in the system and minutely portioned out. Rare and curious historical accretions encrust the entire grand edifice.

The technical aspect of information flow within the Church involves a strong directional tendency. Most doctrinal innovation or clarification moves downward from above, sometimes with accessory flows from special studious bodies, technical and legal agencies, councils, and commissions. On occasion, universal councils like the recent one convened by John XXIII for *aggiornamento* have met to settle points of doctrine, often at the cost of permanently alienating the losing minority. When centralism too directly challenged the dignity and freedom of a local hierarch, anathemas and schisms would frequently ensue.

The conduct of religious ceremonies and the rules of public and private morality expounded by the Church likewise originate at the upper levels, and are disseminated throughout the structure. Individual choice and conscience, we must remember nonetheless, represent the real focus of Catholicism, for the Church regards its mission as that of enlightening the free will of mankind, and considers every man's responsibility for his own salvation as inescapable. Enlightenment and guidance from above, however, manifest themselves much more strongly in the Catholic Church than in most other religious bodies.

Catholicism, as the name implies, aspires to true universality, and the Church accommodates a greater breadth of belief, ritual practice, and forms of governance than laymen ordinarily conceive. Beside the secular clergy, i.e., the parish priest and the officers directly over them, the "regular" religious, those who follow a certain rule of religious life and devotion, represent many different monastic orders with highly diverse charters and charges. They contrast markedly among themselves, for example, in their attitudes toward missionary work, and in their relationships with local bishops. Then too, the Church enfolds within its jurisdiction many congregations other than the Latin. Ancient oriental patriarchates affiliated with Rome parallel their unassociated brethren; Greek, Chaldean, Jacobite, Syrian, Coptic, Slavonic, and yet other rites and forms within the embrace of the Catholic whole continue ancient local traditions. Some of these Eastern Rite affiliates, such as the Maronite and Ruthenian, serve very considerable populations, and in spirit and discipline stand quite far apart from Roman ways (e.g., in permitting clerical marriage and in celebrating distinct feasts). The Church also accords more autonomy to certain national hierarchies within the Western Latin branch than is commonly supposed, so that, for instance, the Spanish state controls the elevation of bishops, the Dutch hierarchy countenance a notably broad spectrum of theological views, and different feasts and devotions prevail in almost every country.

The history of Catholicism's establishment, too, exemplifies general patterns in the geographic development of such institutions. An inspired or divine figure—savior, prophet, buddha—appears among men under miraculous or marvelous circumstances, often singling out a special people for his mission. He early displays his supernatural powers, and soon embarks on a teaching mission among the multitudes. His charisma attracts adherents and disciples far and wide, and when he passes from the scene, they continue to observe his teachings and venerate his person. Then they begin to consolidate and expand. Thus, after Christ died, the communities of early Christians, mostly anchored in the little settlements of Jews around the East, went on meeting and admonishing each other toward the righteous way. They soon found a guide and standard in the letters and visits of energetic, capable men like St. Paul. The organized body thus emerged from local congregations welded together by these later apostles. It became, after many vicissitudes, an irresistible force in Roman society, and finally achieved official preference.

Christianity had to contend with vigorous rivals for primacy. They included Egyptian magical cults; the Mithraist and Manichaean dualist religions out of Persia, which had gained a strong hold on the armies; and of course the official pagan creed and civic rites of Rome, along with various sophisticated philosophical movements like Stoicism. Persistent, fearless missionary effort, importunately disseminating the creed and recruiting communicants in face of exile, martyrdom, and general harassment, expressed the Christians' concept of their inherent obligation to proselytize, and undoubtedly accounts for the success of their movement in gaining full toleration within the Roman Empire by the reign of Constantine (circa 300 A.D.). Thenceforth, the conversion of Europe, adjacent Africa, and the Near East proceeded rapidly and irresistibly. And as the creed spread thus, disputes inevitably arose over its interpretation, and the Church began to split apart.

The Christian community from the beginning carried on the vigorous Old Testament kind of exclusivism, declaring its antagonism toward competing faiths, and not hesitating at all to stamp them out when it secured official status in the Empire. It grew by sending out or setting up colonies, linked together by the busy travels and untiring correspondence of administrators and preachers, and soon apportioned the localities among bishoprics. The scattered nodes of the faithful, linked by long, obscure lines of communication, began to transmute into an entire, dense domain, whose towns became the seats of the growing hierarchy.

Tradition remembers the epochal efforts of the missionary monks of Europe to establish dialogue with the native heathens and to integrate new areas into the network and territories of the Church. Saints like

Patrick, Boniface, Cyril, and Methodius, actual or legendary, exemplify these heroes. Their work in Europe terminated only in the fifteenth century with the conversion of the pagan Lithuanian tribes, just when Christian missionaries were setting out again to convert freshly discovered overseas worlds. Elsewhere, the faith percolated slowly southward in Africa along the Nile, eventually to reach remote native kingdoms that cherished it for centuries in isolation. Levantine monks took their religion into Iran and the deserts of Central Asia, and southward into India. Despite the collapse of central unity in Christianity and the incursions of Islam, the results of these achievements were never quite blotted out in Africa and Asia.

Meanwhile, at the core, ferment and dissension caused a series of embittered separations that brought about the establishment of rival Christian hierarchies throughout the eastern world. Out of querulous councils emerged the separate Armenian Apostolic Church, the Monophysite Coptic Churches of Egypt and Ethiopia, the Nestorian Church of the East ("Assyrians"), the Jacobites of Syria, and the several Eastern Orthodox groups—Greek, Palestinian-Greek, Bulgarian, Serbian, Georgian, Romanian, Syriac, Russian, Ukrainian, Albanian, and others, each becoming self-governing at some later time. Rival patriarchs, sometimes two or three in the same city (e.g., Antioch), ruled different flocks and defied all assertions of Roman paramountcy. Like languages, the doctrines and procedural rules that grew to differ so widely expressed a general dialectic tension, carrying in themselves the seeds of destruction for the single institution.

Christian Church councils debated at length over abstruse theological issues and ecclesiastical regulations without ever attaining full agreement. Such was the expectable result of the tendency to local interpretation and, occasionally, local improvisation within so far-flung a system. Furthermore, even the monastic orders that arose in response to prevailing despair at the state of the world, or out of zeal for further converts, deviated from the established patterns according to their own needs and circumstances. Their special regimes entailed new views of things and sometimes asserted an almost insubordinate autonomy that Popes and bishops did not welcome. Likewise hermits, holy men, crusading preachers, and miracle workers continually arose to plague and embarrass the sedate establishment. Earthy rituals, surviving from the days of paganism, superstitions drifting in from infidel sources, divination, witchcraft, and diabolism ate away at the purity of faith and morals.

Geographically, these processes expressed several conjoint tendencies. One was the splitting of the Christian world into a number of different hierarchical systems, each with its independent net of communications. Ferociously at odds, these bodies each laid claim to mutually exclusive but generously overlapping areas, with unfortunate results for border zones. Furthermore, the internal realms of each new entity, particularly the vaster ones, began themselves to undergo the process of local dif-

29

ferentiation, reflecting the poor state of most communications in those times, as well as indicating that pre-Christian traditions had begun to reassert themselves. The dissolution of the unitary Christian domain, always more ideal than actual, proceeded briskly; characteristically, however, it did not then result in total disappearance of all kinship and communion, for the faith was anchored in the landscape and in the language and activity of the people of the Christian lands. The cessation, at a certain stage, of the process of dissociation within the body of believers attests the still effective maintenance of communications, now not territorial so much as familial, not official and extended, but intimate and local. Once implanted in the land and the population, the religion thus took root.

The further history of Christianity in Western Europe saw the rise of new defiances. Wycliffe in England, Hus in Bohemia, the Unitarians in Transylvania, and countless others stood up to challenge the late medieval church. When persistent desire for reform of the increasingly flagrant clerical abuses—venality, simony, nepotism, and general ignorance and debauchery—erupted into open challenge within the Church in the fifteenth century, temporal rulers laid hold of the weapon of indignation against the worldly, wealthy Church and enthusiastically joined the sincere reformers for their own reasons. The overthrow of Roman suzerainty and the evolution of a host of Protestant bodies initiated a continuing subdivision that carried on an old tendency, further comminuting territorial sectors. In the latter days, however, the sects so intricately commingled that no map can any longer do them justice.

Later developments in the religious life of northwestern Europe and America suggest that charisma had become almost commonplace. Sects begat further sects, and never had prophets been so numerous or so minor, yet so effective. The early rival leaders did not hesitate to burn and banish other reformers, and for centuries the persecution of religious dissidents provided a major motive for migrations. At first North America appealed as a haven to the persecuted faithful of stubborn sects, then its Colonies in their turn set about harassing those who did not conform to their own dispensations. The American religious scene displays the leftovers of many reforms and crusades, and missionaries still prowl American streets.

The mechanisms effecting both religious differentiation and religious standardization are even now plainly discernible in any American neighborhood. The fractioning of church bodies continues apace, even despite, and sometimes incidental to, the contemporary ecumenical drive for unification. Mostly, even when two churches do merge, splinter groups of each remain unreconciled, and so out of the two not one but three arise. A more general cause of the ongoing proliferation of religious organizations and doctrines lies in the operations of independent preachers, often vastly popular, over radio and television as well as before brush-arbor and store-front church assemblies. Almost every such ephemeral revivalist expounds his own theology and indulges in a moral and even political brand of evangelism, inspiring a cluster of his followers to form yet another small church. The fundamentalist slum or countryside evangelists are not alone in contributing to this increase of denominations; assorted genteel exponents of spiritualism, mysticism, and occultism join them.

Alongside these manifold agencies of division, the religious congregations in the North American setting exhibit the usual unifying practices. Formal liturgies and the day-to-day functioning of a considerable hierarchy or bureaucracy assure continuity and legitimacy for many of the larger denominations. Both they and, more especially, some of the minority and radical sects also employ special preaching, missionaries on the streets, the distribution of printed tracts, advertising in the press, radio and television "hours," and sometimes even billboards to proclaim their teaching and explain their advantages. Apostolates are many. Indomitable missionaries of the Latter Day Saints, Jehovah's Witnesses, and Soka Gakkai (a Japanese Buddhist import) canvass door to door. All the groups assiduously seek to spread their ways, employing techniques known for centuries, with here and there a novel modern twist. The dissemination and preservation of a dogma still depends upon communication.

Religions of the East

Another epoch began with the dream-revelations of Mahomet the Prophet. Islam, cometlike, flashed out of obscure Arabia and within two centuries had conquered a domain from Spain to Samarkand. The propagation of the religion closely paralleled the spread of Arab military power, although the Moslems ordinarily did not, as some allege, convert all their subject populations at sword's point. The warrior champions of Islam, in any case, have full counterparts in the fighting monks of medieval Christian orders like the Knights of the Sword and the Templars. The rapid, seething spread of the Moslem faith, however, under the aegis of the Arab armies, does contrast with Christianity's much slower and less warlike initial progress.

Islam, as a creed and a way of life, has the declared advantage of great clarity and simplicity. It is readily explained and communicated, and the classical Arabic of the Holy Koran serves as a complete and immutable guide to the faith. The religion apparently first took hold in cities, wherein compact populations of diverse origin must have constituted very favorable media for its propagation. Later it spread through independent desert nomad tribes and among the caravan drivers who served the cities, thus acquiring serviceable vehicles of ready dissemination over enormous distances. But it was principally the army, inflamed with zeal, that carried it in all directions, sweeping all before it. Christian writers often slight the fact that Islam very largely supplanted Christianity wherever the Arabs succeeded in penetrating. The Levant, Egypt and North Africa, Mesopotamia, and much of Iran and Central Asia where it gained a foothold had earlier been devoutly, if disputatiously, Christian. Dissension among schools and sects of Christians, indeed, seems to have prepared the soil well for the implantation of a new religion.

Reaching its apogee in the eighth century, this first phase of Moslem expansiveness then faded, as the heritors of the doughty warriors fell to quarreling and had to relinquish ultimately certain areas, such as Spain, to Christianity. Other Moslem races carried forward later expansions: Seljuk and Osmanli Turks in Anatolia and southeastern Europe; Tatars on the Eurasian steppe and along the Volga; Persians and Afghans into India; Mongols and their confederates to farthest China; Indians, Malays, and some Arabs into distant Indonesia; native Arabs and other local peoples down into Africa. The initial phase installed Islam throughout an area focused on the desert cities; later advances added geographically varied areas such as Bosnia and part of Albania, the middle Volga, some of north- and southwest China, an essentially maritime realm in southeastern Asia (coastal Ceylon, Malaya, Mindanao and Sulu, most of Indonesia), and the southern borderlands of the desert, as well as east coast zones, in Africa.

Perhaps no religious realm exemplifies so well as Islam the role of a fixed source of creed, along with a steady flow of teachers, scholars, and religious leaders throughout the area, in maintaining unity, once conquest and conversion have been achieved. But Islam's hospitality to all men, and its disdain of divisive theological disputation, also worked to keep it uniform. What pilgrims and mendicant friars had achieved in Christianity, the whole active community of believers continued to achieve for Islam. Among them every man is missionary, brother, monk, and messenger. Whereas Christianity is organized, Islam is organic.

But even Islam split, albeit not so wrenchingly as Christianity. Divisions in the body of Islam, at least in theory, do not reflect upon the integrity of the faith or the brotherhood of all the faithful. The areal repartition between the widespread Sunni school and the more restricted Shi'ism of Iran and nearby areas, and the pocking of its wide domain with local variants like the Sufi mysticism of Persia, saint cults of the Maghreb, and Anatolian dervish orders, fail to create a total schism. The explicit priority of koranic sources of tradition, supplemented by written historical accounts and commentaries, ensures a basis for oneness.

The communications-basis of another major religion, Buddhism, lay not nearly so much in unity of dogma as in the *sangha*, or monastic brotherhood of seekers of Enlightenment, who carried the teaching far and wide. Monasteries, not places of public worship or even shrines, are Buddhism's anchors. Yet the course of Buddhist expansion also displayed a generous amount of warlike help. Military conquests by Asoka and his successors spread the doctrine through India, and other warrior kings propagated it in Central Asia. Buddhist monks, however, peaceably infiltrated the mass of Hinduism over much of southern Asia and drifted pacifically over the great mountain ranges into China. In China, and in Korea and Japan whither it was carried onward, the movement underwent persecution at times, and in turn some Buddhist rulers bore down on rival religions. Some later versions of the gentle way incorporated much ascetic, martial harshness.

Penetrating into the interior plateaux and deserts of Asia, Buddhism metamorphosed into a highly differentiated Lamaism, producing numerous contending branches in Tibet and Mongolia. Some of the Mongol factions in particular developed into military orders and periodically engaged in outright warfare with each other. But at least the monkish cast remained wherever Buddha's teaching spread, and both their permeation of so much of Oriental society, and the heterogeneity of outlook and cult among the Buddhist sects—greater even than among the Christian—rest on the undogmatic and devoted influence of the monks. Geographically, Buddhism represents an irregularly distributed array of monasteries exercising variable, and not always notable, influence over the lay people, and forming cores for highly variegated sects. The pattern came about through an expansion reminiscent at times of the monastic phase of Christian growth, but it is maintained infinitely less purposefully than the sway of any Christian sect.

If only for its demonstration of the sheer tenacity of some religious notions, the situation of Iran deserves special mention. Persia has had a troubled but surprisingly consistent, distinctive, and continuous career as a religious entity (and cultural entity in general) even through the Moslem period. One view of the world has dominated there, imposed itself upon (or insinuated itself into) creeds brought in from elsewhere, and periodically diffused in great pulsations over neighboring domains. This is dualism. Ancient Iranian polytheism tracing back to prehistoric times gave rise by Achaemenian times to the official Zoroastrian religion, and the latter lasted as a state religion for at least a millennium. Zoroastrianism (also known as Mazdaism) engendered but survived two world religions, Mithraism and Manichaeism, both prominent in the Roman Empire when Christianity began and both deeply dualistic, emphasizing the contrasts of good and evil, the light and the darkness. Manichaeism especially thrived among the Romans, and it succeeded in implanting itself well enough to crop up even in the Middle Ages, when it surfaced in the Christian world as the movements of the Cathari and Albigensians in Italy and France—both ferociously repressed—and of the Bogomils in Bosnia. But official sanction and protection mostly kept the Mazda version of Iranian religion dominant at home until the triumph of Islam about A.D. 700. Thereafter, increasingly disadvantaged and discriminated against, a reduced Zoroastrian body still remained, and it has in fact persisted in a few communities in modern Iran, as well as among the refugee Parsees of western India. Much later, Iran gave birth to other new faiths in the nineteenth century that coalesced into the now worldwide, synthesizing Bahai. On subsistent, dualistic foundations, a succession of prophets' compelling creeds swept over and out of Iran, the core of the population retaining its old faith for centuries despite them. And at last Islam itself in Persia became affected by the local atmosphere and the Shi'a version of it found its major haven there, as did the mystical and ecstatic school of Sufism.

An even more explicit linkage of religious ideas with a single nation, although not so much a single geographic unit, occurred in the case of Judaism. The doctrines and even ritual practices have changed considerably since early times, but the religion of the Jews continues exclusive, intense, and intact. Even when the Diaspora sent the people to wander over the face of the earth, their unity remained unbroken, thanks in large degree to the deliberate institution of regular correspondence (recalling the early Christian epistolatory connections) among Jewish settlements everywhere, as well as to the travels of teachers and scholars among communities for the purpose of expounding the tradition. The religious teachings of the Jews, like those of the Moslems, were incorporated into sacred books, then into an ever-expanding mass of commentaries on the sacred books, and eventually into commentaries upon the commentaries. A peerless intellectual tradition, as well as a fervent ritual observance and group spirit, came to mark the people. In this instance, apart from the absorption of subject and neighbor tribes enumerated in the Bible, there came only one short period of missionary endeavor. For a time, early in the modern era, Jewish teachers and local rulers actively proselytized, so that converts to Judaism appeared among North African (e.g., Berber and Ethiopian) tribes, Arab dwellers along the Red Sea, Turkic peoples (the Khazars) of the Black Sea region, and no doubt elsewhere. On the whole, Judaism has shown itself content to survive rather than expand, and that feat in itself has entailed great sufferings and remarkable fortitude.

Hindu religion, a congeries of cults and rites, like Judaism presents a "national" aspect, but with infinitely greater ties to actual landscapes. Except intermittently, it has not enjoyed official, much less military propagation, nor has the faith of the people itself borne much relation to the sacred books. Caste, the total organization of society regulating even the minutest habits of daily life, distinguishes the Hindu way. Food, marriage bonds, occupations, residence, festivals observed, and other such key aspects of living obey caste lines. The great and ancient books foreshadow caste, but it goes far deeper; Hinduism is a sociology, not a theology. At one time, Hindu states predominated in western Indonesia, Southeast Asia, and even parts of the Philippines. But overwhelmingly, Hindu religion remains the multifaceted and idiosyncratic expression of life in India itself, immersed in intensely local traditions and even today articulating a whole tremendously complex and diverse society by way of its rules of caste purity.

Within India, particularly Punjab, the Sikh minority professes a militant and exacting faith, marking them as more or less a nation apart. Sikhism arose as an attempt to reconcile Hindu and Moslem where they dwelt adjoining each other. Initially pacifically inclined, it evolved into an outspoken military movement in the crush of animosities and persecutions that early beset it. It now relies on intense family and communal loyalty, and unswerving faithfulness to specific usages and the sacred literature, and does not to any extent seek conversions. Similarly, the Indian Jain religion has become encapsulated after beginning as a missionizing reform movement. Many smaller syncretic religious bodies have similarly arisen where the domains of great faiths met.

The whole rhythm and order of Indian life express and enforce the caste system, the festivals and devotions of the different localities and populations, and the continuing brahmanic ritual and moral leadership. Moslem, Sikh, Jain, Nestorian and Roman Christian—even Jewish—enclaves, some very populous and geographically widespread, occur within the great and heterogeneous body of the Hindu majority.

Some of the lesser religious bodies of the civilized Old World astonish by their hardy persistence. The Parsees and Zoroastrians, already mentioned, still hold out despite repeated waves of religious conversions and hideous persecutions, although now only as vestiges of the once widespread community. A little group of peculiar people, the Mandaeans, tucked away in the northern borderlands of Mesopotamia, apparently preserve the veneration of the stars bequeathed to them by ancient Babylon and Sumer, alongside gnostic elements received from Hellenistic sources. In Syria the Druzes, fierce and secretive dissenters from Islam, like their neighbors the Yezidis, whom surrounding folk accuse of devil worship, live by a religion no outsider fully knows. Along with multiple Christian bodies and Moslem groups and offshoots (e.g., the Alaouites and the Ismaili, or Assassins), these smaller communities contribute to an unparalleled diversity in Middle Eastern religious geography. Their geographic relevance, apart from the ancient and remote connections they exemplify, lies in the very fact of their continuance. Such groups, embattled and closegathered, preserve within their own confines traditions elsewhere lost or extirpated forcibly. Their links with the outside can be only minimal, for they manage to instill in generation after generation a faith and pride so strong, and yet so unlike those of their equally or more fanatical neighbors, that massacres and martyrdoms belong almost to daily life. In much of this crossroad area, the mosaic of such communities remains for some periods stable and tranquil, to be disturbed now and again by such gory outbursts as the warfare of the Druzes against their Maronite Christian neighbors in Syria in the first decades of this century, and the Kurdish slaughter of Armenian Christians at the Turkish regime's behest around the time of World War I. The social and geographic isolation of these minor communities, even with all the vulnerability it implies, hint at a mode of fragmentary preservation that may characterize other cultural features beside religion. The regional arrangement of diversity they exemplify marks as specialized a pattern as the large uniformities of some other Islamic as well as Christian areas. It contrasts with the indiscriminate layering of traditions prevalent in China (simultaneously Taoist, Confucian, Buddhist, even Christian or Maoist), and the caste system of India, which combines social integration with religious differentiation.

Religion Without Books

Many of the religions called primitive may emphatically belie the title; many an observer, antagonistic (like most missionaries) or merely imperceptive, underrates them. The features that inveterately mark such religions, notably their identification with nature in particular small localities, and their lack of written expressions, do not necessarily imply simplicity or backwardness. In fact, their ritual development may excel that of supposedly more advanced religions, and their idea systems can attain both high poetic quality and a keen grasp of natural phenomena and human nature. "Heathenism" contrasts in its localism and concrete rootedness with the world religions, so-called, presenting decidedly different geographical characteristics.

Geographically interesting also because of their intimate association with the day-to-day conditions of environment, many "primitive" religions actually embody a variety of aspects: magic, socially expressive rites of passage, speculative cosmologies, prophecy or divination, ecstatic possession, commemoration of the dead, festivals of thanks, bodily and spiritual purification, instruction of the young. All these elements appear with equal prominence in the great world religions, but the primitives' versions often strike outsiders as either picturesque or wicked. The difference between these shamanisms, idolatries, nature-religions, and such on the one hand, and the great "religions of the book" on the other, amounts however to no more than the fact that the latter carry great standardizing superstructures, imposed on local folk by missionary zeal and conquest. The underlying beliefs and ceremonial observances do not differ all that much from heathenism. The greater differences are not inherent properties, but geographical dispositions and connections.

The areal extent of Christianity, Islam, Buddhism, and the other great faiths, a consequence of their deliberate and fervent propagation, differentiates them, but even in this respect the so-called primitives can show some corresponding examples. Lack of written records precludes knowledge in detail of most of the widespread religious movements that probably occurred among heathens in earlier times, but preliterate yet advanced cultures such as those of ancient Mexico and of the Mediterranean Basin in the second millennium B.C. have left ample evidence of the spread of great universalistic religions, the particulars of which, except for what graven monuments reveal, have now been lost. The megalithic culture that emanated from some East Mediterranean source and implanted itself on all the western shores of that sea, as well as along the Atlantic littoral of Europe about 2000 B.C., surely represented nothing less than a spreading religious system—something dimly recalled as the "Mother Goddess" or "Great Mother" cult. For another example, the horse cults that manifestly dominated the Eurasian steppe at one time have left evidences in art and in tombs, and historically, annoyed the Christian church in early Europe enough to call down a lasting ban on horsemeat.

In later centuries, religious frenzies, nativistic revivals, and messianic cults have often developed out of the cruel contact between indigenous peoples and intruding Europeans. Late in the nineteenth century, among the western Indians of North America, a series of excited native preachers spread the visionary, eerie Ghost Dance Religion, which promised the expulsion of the Whites and return of the hunters' game. The current spread of the Native American Church or "peyote cult" also represents a nativistic revival that incorporates elements communicated by the Christian faith, and duly alarms the non-Indian.

All areas of so-called primitive religion are subject, quite logically, to such outbursts. Even that most civilized of nations, China, had its Taiping episode. Nativistic movements after all consist of nothing else than the legitimate counterparts of the great religious epochs that produced Christianity and Islam. The dramatic spread of religious movements constitutes a quite expectable phenomenon of cultural geography. It is only the subsequent failure to survive and standardize that separates the Ghost Dance, for instance, from a world religion.

Geographical Structure of Religions

Any organized religion has geographical patterns of its own. Take the Catholic example again. To begin with, how shall the distribution of the Catholic population itself be described? Communicants, living interspersed with non-Catholics, participate in church functions in varying ways, and more or less regularly; not all invariably obey ecclesiastical decrees. Catholicism simply holds that all persons baptized in the Church are Catholics, no matter how often they hear mass, receive the sacraments, or heed directions from the hierarchy. Many sin in these regards, yet remain members of the Church. Apostasy implies no release from obligations. But membership in any religious body presents formidable ambiguities for anyone who tries to measure it. Intensity or purity of faith, correctness of behavior, frequency of participation, all might serve as indices, but all resist convenient investigation. Thus mapping denominations has its problems.

Assuming uniform and total observance by the laity, the parishes, each centered on a church, form a general geographic fabric. At key points—market or administrative towns, most commonly—are the bishops' palaces or offices. Over and above these stands archdiocesan chanceries in great cities, usually serving several million faithful; over these in turn may preside national congresses and associations of bishops, in national capitals, still beneath the central see at Rome. The structure means little without the linkages informing it, which nowadays coincide with the general connections and public carriers of the respective countries. The Church in the past, however, employed its own system of couriers and agents when appropriate, and still provides special communications where necessary. Encyclicals, papal bulls, and all manner of pronouncements and directives grading down to parish sermons form the content of the flow. Much of the information proper to the celebration of sacred rites, and needed for the spiritual and practical guidance of the faithful, nonetheless, occurs in written form in the reach of every priest. Not all communication in an institution moves; some lies at hand embodied in environments. Artifacts store messages.

Parallel to the regular edifice of parishes and bishoprics, each of the very numerous religious orders has its territorial system. Some highly standardized organizations (e.g., the Jesuits) have schools, novitiates, retreats, and domiciles emplaced at intervals around the Catholic world. Others consist, territorially, of a handful of monasteries connected mainly by the mails and occasional emissaries in person. Some involve themselves mightily in the life of the world, others withdraw entirely into contemplation. Hardly any layman knows of the great number of substantial religious establishments that flourish, frequently half-hidden, in the landscapes of the United States and Canada.

Alongside the foregoing territorial systems occurs another worldwide array consisting of places of devotion—shrines, basilicas, oratories, chapels, tombs—associated with pilgrimage. Pilgrim traffic in Catholicism remains surprisingly vigorous and voluminous. Lourdes, Fatima, Ste. Anne de Beaupré, and Guadalupe attract hundreds of thousands of visitors every year. The work of pilgrims in disseminating ideas (secular as well as religious) and in bringing coreligionists closer together in spirit commands notice. Among them, if anywhere, real unconstrained diffusion can take place.

Sites of Christian pilgrimage like Canterbury, Santiago de Compostela, Valaam, and Mount Athos often have long histories, but the title of oldest and greatest belongs to Jerusalem. Other religions cherish their own shrines and sanctuaries. Ancient Grecian pilgrims went to Delphi or Eleusis. Mecca calls all Moslems, and Karbala in Iraq attracts great numbers of Shi'ite pilgrims. The Ganges and the city of Banaras are focal destinations for the Hindus, as Bodh Gaya in Bihar, where Buddha attained Enlightenment, is for the Buddhist world. Places of local and long pilgrimage alike remain abundant, and millions of persons travel to them every year. Many of them constitute impressive and significant landscape features in their own right.

The geographic panorama of religion, then, embraces a population of believers served sometimes by a hierarchical, territorial body of ministers, and sometimes not; an array of monastic foundations; and a group of holy places frequented by pilgrims. Communication among these agencies avails itself both of ordinary channels, and of their own. But an enormous element in the communication of religious ideas and injunctions rests upon the deliberate, expressive use of landscapes. The imprint of religion and related institutions on most landscapes is tremendous.

Akin to religious bodies in their role as disseminators of information and as territorial entities, other institutions display similar structures. An army, for example, ordinarily consists of units ranked hierarchically and exercising control over designated territorial domains and structures. Within military systems, too, parallel subsystems differentiate themselves: combat units, supply, intelligence, inspection, medical service. Notably, too, an army at war distinguishes operational zones cutting across the sectors belonging to its component units; thus it has a combat zone, a comunications zone, and a zone of the interior behind them. The first may further break down into such areas as no man's land, outpost line, main line of resistance, support and reserve area, and rear. Army units even on the move preserve both hierarchical command distinctions and a spatial order among constituents, and communications among command levels and within units follows carefully prescribed forms. It has gradually dawned on military thinkers that communication is the key to operations; Napoleon Bonaparte contributed the clearest demonstration of this principle in his own strategies. Modern armies therefore invest heavily in the corresponding equipment and facilities. Warfare in some modern contexts has become essentially a struggle over the control of communications, rather than a race for booty or a campaign of systematic extermination.

The Spatial World of Institutions

Bureaucracies of state, like those within a church or military system, consist of great communications networks. The political division of the world into an exhaustive set of national states and dependencies, and the subdivision of each of these into provinces and comparable units, which break down still further in most cases into districts, cantons, counties, or similar areas, exhibits the same principles of jurisdiction and superordination as the other cases. Initiative and control, again, increase upward. Parallel systems accompany such political structures, too; often the towns and cities form a separate, less articulated series, adjunct to the extended areal one. Thus the towns and cities in the United States, Canada, and the Soviet Union stand somewhat apart from the county or the rural *raion* administratively, and have considerable autonomy as well as loose but direct relations among themselves. In an urban age, however, the ill-defined order and chain of authority affecting cities constitutes a handicap to the efficient conduct of public business. Rival jurisdictions assert parity and independence regardless of relative size and importance, e.g., the hundreds of "free and sovereign" jurisdictions in northeastern Illinois, of which Chicago only counts as one. Many areas suffer from a chaos of noncooperating parallel jurisdictions; this patently geographic problem vexes several countries.

Political geography, as a special study of administrative bureaucracies and their geographic relationships among themselves and with their subjects, relates strongly to communication. Equally intriguing for their communications aspects, but even less clearly understood, business and production enterprises also have geographic structures. These commonly consist of hierarchies with territorial extension, and employ a notable portion of their effort for communication. Some, of course, devote themselves only to internal operations that consist largely of collecting and disseminating information. Others manage technical communications for society in general, or conduct a commodity trade. Surely at least some principles applying to the geographical organization of religious bodies or military systems apply to them as well. Individual enterprises have their histories, quite commonly relating to their territorial expansion and even differentiation. Their installations form complete and integrated systems much dependent on coordination. The case becomes especially complex, however, since businesses compete, and many different agencies serving essentially like functions may coexist and overlap in areas. The sort of exclusivism that is dear to religions would delight businessmen, too, but such enforced monopoly is rare. The geography of business embraces development and operation in contexts almost always rich in alternatives and competing pressures, thereby attaining a notorious complexity. The element of secrecy, material more often than not to full success in business, makes access to the details difficult, but the geography of such organizations and their functions in dissemination of information holds a special, distant fascination. Its cultural significance no doubt tends, perhaps because of the special demands of the case, not to receive sufficient respect. Few forces exert more influence on ordinary lives in today's world than organized, large-scale business, whether capitalistic corporations, communist trusts, or state monopolies incarnate it.

Businesses, like religions, states, and armies, occupy themselves to an imposing extent with ritual and symbolism. Both for purposes of achieving and maintaining internal solidarity and obedience, and for securing the attention and custom of the public, businesses commonly portray themselves dramatically in external symbols and pageants. Their premises represent their merits and their magnates' genius, and thereby become the private equivalents of temples dedicated to divinities. Their panoplies can dominate whole cities.

Before turning to this topic of the messages in landscapes, notice the human implications of the matter. Institutions stand for something vital in our lives, and each of these great systems, with its busy linkages, exemplifies that factor. Recognized as beings in their own right, almost analogous to living persons, with individuality and character like people, and with histories and lives, institutions patently partake of a moral existence. They express or exemplify values. Their values in turn derive from the actions and characters of men who, through institutions, manifest them. Thus for instance a religion is a sum of lives lived meaningfully.

Binding people together in a great and lasting body, seeking more than petty private ends, exemplifying nobler values, institutions allow expression of inner voices. They provide careers, round out identities, encompass worthy destinies, and promise a commemoration. Or construe their role another way, as an interminable drama in which men find their parts and earn their credit. Their design is like a map for life's progression. But men rarely sense the full portent when they make choices, and so they seldom progress far, yet still their membership has given bearings to their lives. And somewhere on the earth, the signs of their existence have been planted to last amid the works they helped create.

Clearly not mere inclusion within an institution, but participation in activity, gives definition to a life. Constant dialogue and expression occupy participants—their mutual intelligibility arises from the agreed historic premises embodied in the institution, with merit, dignity, and satisfaction hinging thereon. All the ongoing business, the dialectic bustle of contending novelty and precedent, emanates from living. At root an institutional order follows simply from vitality. But human beings, sometimes engrafted into many institutions simultaneously, participate accordingly in several lives and several destinies; a culture, through the varied forms of life indigenous to it, provides for man a multiplicity of pathways.

The world retains the mark of men's expressions through their institutional endeavors. An institution expressly, concretely builds a home for life upon its terms by modifying its surroundings to proclaim its presence and its values. Thus do individuals as well find outlets for their being through a disciplined collective medium. The implications of communicative behavior, especially through institutions, are enormous; those arising from the reshaping of the material world (our next topic) under their guidance and impulse to communication are particularly vast and rich.

CHAPTER 4 *expressive*
environment

Communication ultimately depends upon the senses. The individual field of sensory awareness—the immediate environment—conveys whatever information reaches a human being. Whatever form connections take, they all abut upon the sensory receptors. The flows of communication go through the environment as expressive states presented to perception. Definite, deliberate significance inheres in all environments affected by the work of man. Expression there awaits discovery.

Some expressions are enduring and explicit, others ephemeral and ambiguous. Everything about the body is in itself a declaration: slight facial movements, posture, position of the hands, level of the voice, breathing rhythm, body heat and perspiration, skin color, odors, every motion. The language of dress likewise states its messages, as do the character of a man's possessions generally and the way he keeps and uses them. An American's house and car figure prominently in defining him socially. And the products of a person's actions, read carefully, reveal him. Everyone's style in handiwork, like everyone's face, footfalls, or handwriting, remains distinctive. All these things lie just below deliberate and voluntary levels of communication. Words and deeds in their turn, intentional and expressly used, carry more messages. Some, however, can be deceptive or erroneous without the attendant, subliminal revelations of the body. The discursive order to which verbal communication belongs can say a lot, but far from everything necessary. Still, in poetic use even word-language loses its hard and fast quality and soars free to do miracles. From the highest achievements of art to the daily work of humble toilers, a quality of human meaning attaches to mankind's activity and becomes accessible to those who seek its signs. Far beyond discourse lie the meanings, unspeakable therefore but concrete and unmistakable, that pervade a painting or a work of music. They may occur at multiple levels, and variously; a song recalls natural sounds, a painting exposes a story, only vaguely related to its deeper purposes. Art captures modes of vitality and conveys absolute states. In less purified guises, vitality declares itself around everyone, informing the man-made environment. Even beyond man's own works, nature in general, regarded through lenses of developed sensibility, seems to have "moods" or a "message." A man contemplates his entire surroundings and sees a specious harmony—nature full of clear intention, human works all tending together; the compelling illusion lends more plausibility to existence. Mankind has thus always insisted on perceiving an intended concert in the world; how else could fate be borne?

So in every environment dwells an expressive company: physical, living persons; their many words; and every act and every artifact, embracing all the ways in which man arranges his own things and disarranges nature's. Beside all this, the natural component, as suggested, may seem to bear intended meanings too. Artifacts (and sometimes the arrangements of them, notably in settlements) accuse the identity and style of their makers, and often manifest their own uses and properties. All incorporate a degree of ulterior reference—they are invariably symbols, if only in a small way. Whatever betokens or admits to having a maker, must symbolize him; intelligible signs of use, built-in, must count as symbols of the actions involved. The phenomenon of symbolism, or vicarious meaning, derives from the continuity of life and experience, so that any one environment, any person, any object, any quality of things is capable at times of retrospectively evoking images or values—"responses"— not otherwise possible. It could scarcely mark man off from animals, however, unless the symbol served more than simple recall. A bloodhound tracking a scent, if this were not so, would qualify as symbolusing. A symbol is no accident. It constitutes deliberate and skilled communication; therein lie its special virtue and distinction.

No neat division separates all symbols from the unconscious signals and revelations that people often make, nor do symbols differ altogether in kind from nonsymbolic things. Symbolism is of course a matter of degree, and of particular circumstances as well. Environments include a host of situations, actions, and objects with symbolic content, but not all have equal intensity and clarity. And alongside symbolism range the unpremeditated, artless, giveaway signals like eye-movements and blushing, as well as a good deal of purely circumstantial indication of significance. These latter elements are those things around a person which, having been experienced as limitations and imperatives, constrain him to a restricted choice of action. Environments always infringe on freedom, not only because of prevailing "laws of nature" but also on account of man-made features. Such things communicate through action, but to the perceptive may carry a symbolic value too. Think of a bridge, localizing the operation of stream-crossing, but also embodying its broader suggestiveness.

The symbol serves communication as a vicarious presence. In normal use, however, many artifacts simply function as neutral or nearly neutral vehicles for communication, i.e., signaling devices. Technical media of communication belong in this category, e.g., books and television sets. The work of art, a presence in its own right, claiming an individuality almost personal and disdaining mortality, partakes of some of the character of a symbol, and also of another kind of expression. The unities so fundamental to artistic expression somehow show analogy to the unity of the person who, however he may behave and whatever repertory of expression he may employ, remains identified as himself, conditioning thereby whatever he may enact (e.g., a nun who swears is simply not convincing).

Significance in Settlements

In order to envision how and what environments express, consider settlements, the arrangement and enrichment of environment by man. The shapes and character of settlements, in wonderful diversity, engage attention in that they expose communicative aspects. A settlement means not merely aggregation of a certain number of persons; it involves a specific spatial form, highly differentiated internally as well as sharply set apart from neighbor settlements. Also, it embodies within its social universe a certain corresponding apportionment of life- and work-ways. Another of its aspects, connection with the world beyond it, almost always shows a large diversified supply of communication channels reaching it from elsewhere. They serve different formal and informal institutions, impinging differently through them on each individual in the settlement. Accordingly, the further aspect of the settlement as the locus of each individual life, the *world* of the inhabitant, connotes a differentiated lot of outside contacts. All these and other aspects enter into the fundamental character of settlements as systems of habitual communication. Outside connections, inner form, the symbolism concretized in act and artifact—the whole import of environment—converge upon the alert perceiver.

But the settlement does more than stand in testimony of its own existence. Beside manifesting its distinctive form and nature, it compels attention to its physical constraints, and conformity with certain rules and rhythms. The pressures that enforce its ways come less from social regulation than from the very makeup of the settlement as a finite, ordered universe of concrete objects, each with a specific relation to the others. The physical apparatus of a way of life implies that way. For this reason an agreeable sense of strangeness rewards those who visit a new environment and allow themselves to sense the pattern of existence in it. A visitor may find a full participation in the local life and ways beyond his powers, but even the dullest tourist can appreciate the "foreignness" of a different country. The substitution of one population for another in the same locale would present a special and curious test of foreignness. Have the Poles who moved en masse in 1945 into Pomeranian and Silesian cities since undergone some adaptation to the built-in Germanness of the streets and buildings they inherited?

A settlement communicates its way of life implicitly, whether or not it can be otherwise described. Yet the forms taken by the constraints and cues that guide the way of life are shaped by someone's work, itself obeying rules and styles. The form of the settlement is a command from the past. It expresses and insists upon a certain cultural pattern. Accordingly, it can be regarded as a highly important communication, among the most fundamental of all, connecting the inhabitants at any time with many generations of their predecessors. The surroundings in which a man lives thus contain long-prepared lessons and directions for activity.

The settlement, absolute context of life, constitutes a heritage and so has a history. Its inner synergism, reconciling and amplifying selected basic principles, derives from slow and long adjustment. A kind of convergent evolution operates, in the course of which some themes become submerged and others crystallize out of experience and circumstance. Thus the deep foundations of life that a settlement communicates become imperceptibly modified from generation to generation; it does not remain a static order. Traced back into its remote beginnings, a given settlement of any age will seem to have developed into something very different from its origins, and human settlement in general, over the millennia, undoubtedly has metamorphosed. The great Western cities that today appear to stand primarily for manufacture, commerce, and administration—and which, even more than that, represent great concentrated places of consumption—when compared with those of medieval Europe or the Antique world, betray a special evolution that has modified the older forms.

A thoroughly naive impression of the city, gained just from looking at its skyline, reaches deeper toward its true nature than does sophisticated study of its economic and political order. The pride and power nakedly displayed in shining towers say it all. Utilitarian considerations might explain the present functions of a city, and even aspects of its form, but they do justice neither to its historical nor to its aesthetic side, and incidentally to this, they slight the palpable human import of a city, known to everyone in his own experience.

Although no neat and sure account of city origins is likely ever to be possible, we do possess some glimmering idea of them. The earliest cities, which emerged about 3500 B.C. in Mesopotamia, had no apparent predecessors, and the immediate circumstances of their rise remain unclear. The evidence does show, however, that their rise did not take place just gradually over a wide area in response to uniform and widespread practical demands. The anatomy of these ancient cities offers contrary clues. Temples of the gods invariably dominated, as well as the slightly later palaces of divine kings, along with granaries, garrisons, and other related buildings. For the most part the rest was village, for the cultivators lived within the walls. Both New World and Old World furnish indications of early cities' having combined a rather ordinary village with an opulent collection of palaces and temples. Ceremonial rather than practical beginnings must almost certainly account for city origins. Urban places still have a certain tone of reverence and splendor, no matter how banal or squalid they actually are. And as a rule they command a modicum of loyalty and devotion from their inhabitants, despite their all-too-frequent faults. Every city, even the most humdrum, tries on occasion to stage festivals and functions that redeem its prevailing tedium. As seats and centers of institutional life, too, cities profit from a borrowed pomp and color. Manufacturing and merchandising only overshadow, rather than outshine, these other roles of cities.

Industry at the household scale must surely have existed long before any semblance of industrial cities did, and trade no doubt antedates any kind of urban market. The former function, once well dispersed in residential locations, belongs to almost all societies. The latter almost universally exists between, as well as within, societies. Both industry and trade entered into the life of the most ancient cities but, contrary to the inference from recent cases, clearly had no primary place in them. A purely mundane, practical origin in this sense remains altogether out of the question. As for administrative and military functions, these again betrayed their presence clearly in the venerable cities we know as Uruk, Lagash, Ur. But over them loomed the majesty and awesomeness of city gods whose cult was the core of the urban existence, and whose property embraced the entire domain, its tenants acting as their servants and slaves. The city was a home of gods before it was a home of men.

The evolution of settlement around shrines and tombs, which may be implied in this interpretation, would not be inconsistent with what is known of more recent conditions elsewhere in the world. Markets in particular associate with holy places. The medieval parish churches of Europe still have their market squares, and in many little towns the country people still appear one day a week to buy and sell and gossip. The great cathedral squares also used to harbor markets, even if now they have turned into parking lots. The periodic markets of China, serving the whole countryside on a rotating basis, seem to show some correlation with the towns that had major temples or seats of the imperial cult. In Mayan lands today, the great market days among the dispersed population occur in connection with religious feasts, celebrated in the "empty town" churches with due concurrence of great crowds. Moroccan saints' tombs attract pious visitors on certain great days and markets spring up in conjunction. The connection, so persistent and widespread, would seem to suggest a very ancient pattern.

Did cities, then, evolve from cult-centers into business centers? Perhaps; the significance of "business" represents the issue here. If purely rational and necessary, the business side of cities does indeed *supplant* an older ceremonial role. But do not those older, indisputable associations of the city with religious ceremonial suggest an obvious conclusion, namely that the role of business in our modern lives incorporates a great component of the ceremonial? In this respect, a further patent characteristic of cities throughout history deserves mention. It was not long before the scribes who pullulated in the temple cities found occasion to allude not only to the might of the gods, but also to the exploits of their champions, the warrior kings. Soon the kings began to rival the gods, and then became divine themselves. To this day, men in power seek to commemorate themselves by adorning cities with their palaces, erecting statues to themselves, endowing temples and civic works, opening great imposing avenues and squares, constructing walls and bridges, and otherwise embellishing and expanding their capitals. Today, the urban ornaments depend on wealthy civic figures, and work-places have become the chief memorials to private glory. Public agencies themselves endow yet other staggering constructions. The city still is pride and power.

The religious concept that infused the ancient city always embodied the vision of an ideal way of life. Each city represented the attempt to realize an earthly environment in which that perfect life could be lived. In ancient times the prevailing idea revolved around ritual and worship, so that the city itself, with its sacred gates, processional avenues, broad echeloned pyramids, mystic gardens, and sanctuaries and sacrificial altars, must have been a kind of stage for the continuous enactment of sacred episodes. Cities today also express an idealistic vision of life. Great architectural writers spell out very clearly the assumptions underlying this expression, indeed asserting that improved design would automatically improve the state of society and perhaps even the dispositions of individual people. The architect's dream finds an echo in the suppositions that guide the planners who anticipate and direct change. But such men continue something ancient; the very layout and design of cities everywhere reflect the venerable ancestry of modern planning. Sumerian cities grouped around the great religious and royal edifices; the politicized Greek and Roman cities, focusing on forum- and temple-crowned hills; the medieval European city cowering beneath cathedral spires; the grandiose baroque cities with their spiderweb of avenues and squares— all are closely related to a particular conception of life and to its realization in their frameworks. In other cultures of the past, similar urban patterns have correlated with the ideal order and with life-ways. The massive walled cities of Peru, their full import denied to us by time and silence, still bespeak a life and spirit of their own. Tenochtitlan in Mexico amazed the invading Spaniard with its splendor and vitality, articulated around its pyramids, courts, canals, and lakes and steeped at every point in ritual usages. So it was with the Chinese cities, their nuclei perpetuating camps of conquerors, and civic shrines serving ancient native rites. In several features, cities everywhere today conform to certain basic principles whose origins are almost lost in history. The now-predominant rectangular grid of streets has been shown to go back to Sumer, and seems to express a sacred principle. The custom of letting church steeples tower over other buildings, still prevalent in the last century, asserts itself in the skylines of European villages and American small towns to this day. In larger towns, public power defers only slightly to religion, so that Midwestern courthouses rise almost as high as the highest Christian spires of the towns. But in modern cities the skyscraper has risen to proclaim the accession of enterprise to sovereign precedence. No better statement of change could be found, perhaps, than the Imperial Palace buildings in Tokyo, dwarfed by new hotels and office buildings, and St. Paul's Cathedral, London, brooding in the shadows of American-owned glass and steel.

Every town and village tends to conform in its own rudimentary way to these same principles of expression through design. Regularities and priorities in both layout and profile survive even in the most squalid backwaters. Another feature of expressive and directive character prevails even more noticeably, however. A building belongs, after all, to some person or institution, and stands on someone's land. The whole actual as well as ideal shape of a settlement's life observes the pattern set out in land tenure. Each person's fate remains somehow bound with his appointed place. He conducts his work within spatial limits that divide off his domain but also articulate it with all others. His connections with his own and alien societies fasten there.

The division between the public thoroughfares and private lands tends, notoriously, to become almost ineradicably fixed. Street grids live long. Furthermore, property boundaries in many cultures hardly ever change, although individual parcels may combine within large holdings. Field-lines and their markers, too, last long, so that in many places both roads and fields actually boast names, ancient and individual. The individuality of land transcends particular regimes of property, for even where communities hold it jointly, the parts have separate existences and often names. Each specific, persistent boundary stands for a social as well as geographical distinction.

The Context of Identity

A set of land boundaries encompasses the lives of any family, clan, or other corporate group. The cultivator's field becomes the symbol of

49

himself. His neighbors judge him by the care he gives it and by the crops it yields him. His passion for enlargement of his dignity translates itself into an ambition to enlarge his properties. But man also seems to require a home, a clearly defined, inviolable shrine of his selfhood. No need to look for complicated motives or special inner drives: the continuity and consistency of a life, the ability to learn and apply techniques of survival successfully, need a corresponding regularity of context. This rule pertains as much to social relationships as it does to work which engages men with nature.

As everyone knows, selfhood resides not just in a body. The self derives its identity out of particular rhythms, places, actions, and appearances. No person is real without his plausible setting, his manner and style, his schedules, itineraries, and associations. The need for a place, for a rootedness, is much more than a psychological quirk. Place, person, time, and act form an indivisible unity. To be oneself, one has to be somewhere definite, do certain things, at appropriate times. Accordingly, every place carries in it the implication of a person, of someone's pride and striving, and moreover of a heritage passed down from person to person, continued for each generation's tenancy. Sometimes a forgotten history lurks somewhere, so that a litter of obsidian chips remaining from a prehistoric workshop remembers unknown artisans, and the moving shades of Indians infest the woodlands and desolate valleys of America.

Self will manifest itself in action. Some animal displays are slightly reminiscent of the human way. In defending territory and in courting mates, various species exhibit impressive, ritualized threat behavior. Rival cocks puff up and strut their plumage; bucks flourish awesome antlers. But such ornaments, and all the odd performances that go along with them, have evolved upon genetic bases, and remain inherent and unvarying within each species. They hardly allude to individuality at all, and surely to nothing like selfhood as such. Human beings, on the other hand, express their selfhood in displays they choose themselves. Not just the courting performances of man, which sometimes take such odd directions, but all the tireless meddling of an individual with his environment incorporates display behavior. Men are surely nature's greatest showoffs.

A satisfactory exhibit or performance must assume an audience. Even our "animal" satisfactions have social overtones. Human display is always geared to appreciative and informed witnesses and critics, and thereby its exercise involves all people deeply in some social universe. The utter dependence of creativity of any sort upon a comprehending audience forces adherence to, and in fact virtual submergence in, a particular group. The most secret, solitary enjoyment of one's own strength or skill is, in a way, a borrowed delight. And since what men appreciate in the displays of their fellows (like what the grouse sees in the rituals of other birds) very much depends on group agreement, nothing can leave an individual more forlorn than trying to express his claims to worthiness and attractiveness before an alien audience that cannot read his display. In order for action and its fruits to count as valuable and to justify and glorify their author, they have to conform respectively to some accepted pattern of desirable activity or some class of admired artifact, and lend themselves to critical evaluation. A display must therefore bear some fairly obvious relationship to what the group already knows. The admirable is currently designated, accurately, as "groovy," while the peak of permissible novelty is quite properly called "far out." Action and creation have to retain some congruence with their environments. Total novelty is meaningless.

What consternation people feel when exposed to unfamiliar performances! The Japanese were scandalized, during the Allied Occupation, by American soldiers who engaged in unrestrained public kissing. Latin drivers, engrossing themselves in flourishes their cultures encourage, petrify more cautious Anglo-Saxon passengers. Almost everyone has at least secretly experienced disgust when brought into accidental proximity with some foreign gathering absorbed in a performance after its own unfathomable manner. The steely cheerfulness of early-rising Germans; the noisy, odorous repasts of some other Europeans; the indomitable insensitivity and tastelessness of Yankees—all are amply deplored by other groups. The allegation of uncleanliness almost always crops up against members of an unfamiliar or unwanted group, referring of course to the supposed environments their habits create. (Americans deserve to know that Japanese, Arabs, and Frenchmen consider them, in different, very delicate respects, distressingly unclean.)

A personal display, the environmental manifestation of an individual's claim upon his own self-respect and upon his fellow men's notice, demands a large, in fact an overwhelming portion of his time and effort. The whole shape and story of a life depend upon the strategies and settings chosen for display. Hard livelihood, admittedly, imposes its demands, but even the grubbiest existence has to have its quota of pretensions. No one lives simply a calculated life of pure material sufficiency, without a whit of vain display. Sobriety and thrift and toil themselves are vain, as saints have known; a miser, after all, has got a reputation. Everyone in some degree conforms to circumstances given by environmental heritage and cultural traditions, which will measure him. Everyone competes with his ancestors as with his companions to do as well as they in what is given him to do. The great majority of men need hardly pause to ask what roles they have to play; the few who freely choose face dreadful risks—and may achieve great things. Yet even in the humblest place, variety remains. The social context always throbs with passion and tingles with fantasy, so that any man may plunge into dramatic and original performances or exploits. Evanescent feats and graces constitute most men's display. Most folklore and legends, indeed, have to do with lively, memorable action, not with more enduring creations. But most of mankind achieves self-expression in the less exciting daily work ordained by circumstance and custom.

Nonetheless, expressions cannot fail to differ, depending on the place and people. Environments themselves confer a great variety of roles upon participants in society, and either contrasting environments or distinct societies make for entirely unlike complexes of roles. The real or simulated cowboy context exemplifies different American values and creates different heroes than does the downtown office-worker world. English officers and gentlemen among the colonial natives dressed for dinner, but they would have been astounded had the natives done so. Some closely related cultures esteem very different displays. A South American will pride himself inordinately on cheerless bedroom conquests. The Frenchman sometimes strikes a foreigner as totally obsessed with eating; French tourists almost completely shun countries reputed to produce a poor cuisine. Germans identify intensely with their houses, scrubbed relentlessly and guarded by huge fierce dogs. These stereotypes, while exaggerated, are hardly groundless.

What is home? Surely it is one's display, the setting and the text of life, familiarly felt. And likewise, inseparably, it embraces the company of culture-sharers, those of the same heritage who are conscious of and compassionately critical of one's self-expression. No one can really leave home. Wherever a person goes, he either seeks an audience for comprehension or assumes appreciation *in absentia* of his effort and possessions by appropriate home folk. Real "aliens" are lost souls. Alienation leaves one feeling unperceived, spiritually homeless, bereft of motivation. But the exile remembers home values, and lives in their light.

A promised land, a new home, confers a kind of rebirth on the self, inviting creativity to submit to new criteria. Even the fleeting moments of what we call "recreation" place us in alternative contexts, subject us to new judges and new rules, so the self can take fresh bearings. As modern life becomes crammed with the irrelevance and mutual hermetic incomprehension that accompany bigness and mobility, recreation grows in importance. A man is always losing his selfhood and meaning—in the subway, on the army base, even at home before the awful Box. Recreation of some kind is needed: a saving environment.

By the same token, the most crushing experience of all, unmerciful chastisement, is imprisonment. A prisoner must sit and listen. His self is gagged and bound; he cannot freely manifest his being. Communication forfeited, he wastes. The defiant one, when captive, becomes outnumbered and outgunned; superior force is always brought to bear against him and his confederates. The captive lawbreaker loses his strategic initiative; likewise, he also automatically loses command of the vehicles of self-expression. Perhaps his criminal activity embodies his particular display and claim for notice; it is well known that the skillful and courageous criminal enjoys great admiration and respect from fellow criminals, and even from many police.

All display does not, by any means, remain restricted to the individual. In fact, in many societies, the freest and therefore fullest kinds of expression available to individuals consist of representation made through the family. What could more properly express "pride and joy" than children? The house, too, as well as a few major possessions exhibit the taste, powers, and skills of the family. Such anchors of identity transcend generations, and accumulate significance over the centuries. To possess a house, in such instances, confers great responsibilities to both predecessors and descendants. The care of an inheritance so entrusted weighs on the tenants. A man's castle, be it cave, tent or mansion, receives lavish attention. Whereas individuals find unique expression, personally, in acts and excellences of a transitory sort, what they invest in a family endures. And so, also, do the members of a community resident together, both as individuals and as families, seek to contribute something lasting to the home of the group. For a settlement represents more than an accidental collection of single households—it has a collective identity.

Communal undertakings bring together the families of a place for common ends: to apportion lands among families, provide water and other utilities, make and maintain roads, erect public buildings, create burial grounds, establish shrines and places of worship. The settlement lives in communal efforts despite the several separatenesses it harbors. And the acknowledged common fate and identity have their own expressions in symbols and other display. Zeal for communal expression, of course, extends to larger entities as well, manifesting itself at certain regional levels (e.g., Swiss cantons and American states), and in connection with religious groups, language communities, and the like. People identify with others under many different forms, at many different scales. The sense of human solidarity apparently craves a variety of expressions.

Marks of this tendency to express common spirit are not hard to discern in most landscapes. All conceivable media take part. Sculpture, placards, banners, buildings, and boulevards proclaim the group identity. Music, uniforms, and parades stir patriotic feelings. A smaller element may choose to rest its pride in righteousness and purity, and so develop in its landscapes chaste and stern reminders of its virtues. The Amish communities of Pennsylvania and the Lake States, unworldly and unmechanized, live a demonstration of their principles, visibly eschewing motor vehicles, modern dress, and everything belonging to the alien secular world. Chinese immigrants, wherever able, cluster together amid ample tokens of their difference, and the force of their attachment shows in the generations-long persistence of their separate cityscapes and lifeways. The larger, national entities dwell engrossed in their own histories and their own destinies, of which sufficient reminders commonly exist in their environments. Museums of patriotic art and relics, historic buildings, colorful folk arts, battlefields and national shrines receive particular devotion and emphasis. Practically any country can offer an impressive geography of national symbols of its own. Venerable glories resound in the landscapes of Egypt, Greece, Anatolia, Mesopotamia, Persia, India, Cambodia, China, Mexico, and Peru. Mementoes of the medieval age confer a certain eminence on European countries. Other countries find their pride in frontier epics, appropriately symbolized, as in the cowboy and the gaucho. Each has some sufficient treasure of collective symbolism.

Sometimes a social institution that cannot rule sovereign territory still takes care to register, in some particular environment, its own identity and value. Religious bodies do so most prominently. The Vatican, with its numerous basilicas, squares, chapels, and administrative buildings, displaying all the pageantry of Swiss guards, papal knights, and assorted colleges of foreign clergy, and putting on a constant round of sumptuous ritual exemplifies the splendor if not the power of the Church. So also the holy places of Mecca provide a compelling symbol of the great power of Islam over men's hearts and hopes, when the faithful from all the world congregate for the annual pilgrimages. A respectable variety of mother churches and world headquarters of religious bodies occurs even in the United States, each striving to assert the dignity and worthiness of its community. The sensitive observer might notice subtle differences in tone and tenor of the microlandscapes the various communities choose to represent themselves. Some are pompous, some are plain; some rigid, some relaxed.

Panoplies of group display assert themselves in every landscape. To reiterate a key point, corporate business organizations or major state enterprises claim most notice in contemporary settings. Much as the stately statuary of Paris still honors the great men of literature, the modern cityscape commemorates the big men of business. The lives and strivings recorded in a city's skyscrapers justly correspond to and proclaim the values of the time. Public habit does further reverence to the builders by referring to major buildings under personal or corporation names. The fact that more buildings in recent years have risen to the glory of corporations than to the glory of individuals, affords a diagnostic insight into social trends. This corporate or private pride asserted in tall buildings contrasts with the civic pride encoded in the names of artists, scientists, and benefactors, but far more commonly of politicians, studding public parks, boulevards, reservoirs, auditoriums, sports arenas, airports, and bridges.

Some problems occur in attempting to explain environmental expression. What drives or motives lie behind it? Granted that individuals, families, local communities, religious bodies, businesses, and nations all exert a deliberate and distinctive influence on their surroundings, so as to claim attention and respect: can the same cause suffice for all of them? It might be tempting to invoke some doctrine of motivation, derived from supposed inner tendencies in man, but a simpler argument will fortunately suffice. An individual can be secure only in knowing his own tested limits. Then, too, an individual or group, in order to survive and prosper, needs to articulate with others around, heeding territorial claims and individual temperaments, and exploiting potentialities either left open by neighbors or engendered by their interactions. Alert to the environment, any organism proceeds by trial and error, responding even if haphazardly to immediate pressures. It must somehow adjust or die. Human beings have to react to the same sort of ineluctable necessities. But the enormous complexity of human social life, and the vast technical powers of man, enter into the case. So many factors have to operate together, so much needs integrating and coordinating that the intricacies of even a decidedly primitive village society and its environmental relationships defy analysis. If human beings could not elaborately manifest themselves and all their particular attributes and intentions, it is hard to imagine how they might avoid collision and chaos, which would soon eradicate the species. The simplest viewpoint to adopt interprets man's expressiveness, through symbols and otherwise, as a kind of super-radar used for navigating as if in perpetual dense fog, among interminable shoals and reefs, in a rickety fleet of uncounted thousands of ships close together—and all of the ships, to come through, must depend on the others.

Expressive environments, then, represent the only possible kind of environment for true humanity to live in. It hardly calls for explanation, since the considerations just advanced appear to explain quite readily the absence and impossibility of any other kind of authentic Homo sapiens than an expressive one. But it still remains to ask what environment says, that is, what people actually tell one another through environmental expression.

Environmental Media

Environmental modification has the important consequence of setting out inescapable patterns of future behavior. It bequeaths limits. Once a road becomes laid out, traffic deviates from it only with great difficulty. Routes acquire permanence when accordant property lines come into existence, when people erect walls, fences or hedges, when houses are sited. So traffic, even if uninfluenced by "habits" of its own, capitulates to necessity and follows the road. This principle applies to countless facilities and articles of use. The physical layout of a settlement or a house, and the physical shape of a tool, impose rules. They say "here," "now," or "thus," and that is enough to govern ordinary actions.

Another sort of content in expression hinges on rhythm. Continuance at familiar tasks may seem almost easier than stopping. Spontaneous responses to cycles of community life, as well as acquiescence to imperious bodily rhythms, impel people to perform at their turn or as part of the concert. What is not, as it were, graven into the material body of environment inheres in its temporal shape—a very real element. Rural life inveterately finds itself regulated both by the life rhythms of crops and animals in relation to the seasons, and by the human life cycle and subsidiary body rhythms. The purely mechanical rhythms of a great city, too, can impose themselves on individual lives. Waking and sleeping are more closely governed by the noises of environment than most people think, and probably even appetite, mood, and general health reflect them. Churchbells used to signal the time, and no one misinterpreted their meaning, much less questioned it, but somehow city sounds do not enjoy the same credibility. Mere expression of vitality in itself certainly counts for something in coordinating the life of people living close together. Abundant and telling vital signs surround us all; surely they guide us.

Along with inherent vitality and established form as vehicles of meaning, a whole world of interpersonal expression of a more explicit kind encircles everyone. Its content escapes any finite description. The catalog of meanings has to overflow at this point. But all the meanings people proffer to each other in their interchanges, let it be remembered, take their coloration from the context. Environments invariably assert themselves in the guise of a kind of further grammar of action that determines what interpretation to attach to any given expression on a particular occasion. Circumstance implicitly conditions every declaration.

One further element in most environments carries rich expression: devices expressly used for storing coded meaning or transmitting it. True "communications media" include inscriptions, books, and all things written; to some extent at least all ritual and rote performance; all pictographs and paintings; and the company of modern signal instruments. Again, the contexts count, but less perhaps than in the personal encounter. The relative impersonality of a book or television permits some detachment from the actual environment. Such things have the peculiar effect of releasing a person momentarily from geographical constraints. As the saying has it, they "abolish distance." These media merge, on the one hand, into the universe of art, wherein are realized the most concentrated and refined expressions of all; they adjoin, in another direction, the whole macrogeography of routes of movement and connection among places.

The media just cited, particularly written matter, hold another interest for a geography of expressive environment, namely their capacity for governing action. Since history began the scribes behind the scenes have governed if not ruled. In the China of the mandarins, minute recording and prescription everywhere affected daily life; today they do so universally. Just consider the astonishing and familiar habit of writing all over buildings and landscapes.

Written matter and the neutral vehicles of signal communication generally convey exotic information. They manifest connections, for in most instances they put a locality in touch with the outside, and in the case of books, survive from earlier times as well. Most of the paraphernalia of living nowadays, including but certainly not restricted to those of high communicative potency, come from somewhere else. A substantial exposure to outside ideas and customs therefore results. In the industrial countries, nearly everything a person sees or uses originates among people unknown to him personally, through processes he does not understand. The design and inner workings of his artifacts are unfamiliar. Yet surely many of the objects that surround him carry meanings of some sort, of which a part must be intentional. Import sneaks in unintentionally as well. For example, the characterization of modern life as "plastic" has something deadly accurate about it.

The flood of extrinsic artifacts and continuous exotic communications has become so great in prosperous countries that it seems almost as if "locality" has lost all meaning. Standardizing agencies now operate more widely and effectively than at any other time in history. Households throughout a considerable portion of the world have become crammed as never before with goods from everywhere. The public heed homogenized communications, thanks to electronic media, in a way they previously never could. America is a single city, and Canada struggles not to be its suburb. Especially in the absence of real language barriers, a kind of automatic, unwilled uniformity develops.

The situation does not, however, appear to justify the hasty conclusion that everyone will soon become identical with his neighbor. All the standardizing influences belong to much larger currents of deep social change. New groups and their expressions will arise. Perhaps no better illustration of the fact could exist than the emergence, since about 1960, of large new social movements and political forces in the Western world, attended by considerable stress and violence. As trends toward widespread likeness threatened to engulf the world, obliterating all variety, every country blessed or cursed with mass communication was suddenly wracked with demonstrations, riots, disobedience, and flaunting of the unfamiliar symbols of a new exclusivism. Asian and American, Communist as well as capitalist countries awoke, startled, to a dawning age. As industrial diffusion and communication monopoly proceeded, social dissolution seemed to flourish too. What appears to have developed was a sundering of nearly all advanced societies—as nations grew materially more similar, perhaps—along the lines of age. Geographical variety receded and social division advanced. No doubt the mass communications and homogenized consumption share the blame to some extent, but surely something vastly more profound has been occurring. It would seem as if a principle of age-grading, in particular, has been taking a firm hold on many societies and capsizing old arrangements.

The landscapes of North America, prefiguring those elsewhere, in a substantial form express the realignment of society. Census figures dimly show (and detailed survey would reveal more clearly) that, even as racial segregation diminishes, a process of spatial segregation of residence by age is far advanced. A sizeable proportion of the population over 65 now lives in trailer courts and specialized retirement communities. Their share in the population of warm-winter states and provinces has risen giddily, and manifests itself even in regional politics. On the other hand, housing costs and other factors receive the blame for a noticeable drift of the newly married, childless young into crowded apartments now occupying large continuous zones around many cities. Larger families, coming later, seek the suburbs if they can. The youth now tend to live away from home, if not in college dormitories or military barracks then in hangouts and encampments of their own devising, often even "on the road." An ordinary American or Canadian can now expect, during his lifetime, to migrate every few years from one kind of age-graded settlement to another. The mobility once notorious in North America remained a largely geographic one, affecting families as units; now individuals migrate with their age-peers. And all of this is expressed by the very scenery.

The startling transformation of North America, right in the midst of the consolidation of a single master landscape pattern sprung of mass consumption origins, finds a marvelous expression in the innovative use of many mass consumption artifacts in a way that challenges and supplants intended uses. The arrival of the transistor radio, for example, instead of heralding new triumphs for official communication, ushered in a wave of counter-expression rolling irresistibly along on music, and inundating almost everyone in certain age groups. And the songs that now delight the young, provided courtesy of the unhip corporate boards of recording and broadcasting companies, in many cases boldly advocate protest and defiance of the older mores. An ingenious campaign of symbol-creation, too, has exploited the contents of junk bins and secondhand shops to express new life styles, focused on what not long ago would have been unimaginable pursuits and pleasures. The means of expression employed, exquisitely environmental, from long hair and bare feet to ramshackle collective pads, incense, garish paint, and candles, declare a stubborn autonomy. All this, obviously, links up with the split along age lines, and likewise finds expression in the spatial segregation of the hip community.

Americans ought also to remember that only a generation ago, the "do-it-yourself" craze, accompanying the surge of most of the population for the first time into single-family homes, served as a kernel of defiance against massive standardization and impersonal bureaucratic gigantism. The home in the suburbs—in the endless, uneventful rows of houses in the suburbs—still expresses a poignant urge to manifest one's being in one's own way, after the half-hour on the expressway, after the day on the twentieth floor downtown. For love of freedom, suburbanity gave birth to sadder tyrannies. The independent samenesses of this rebellion, like the hippie "uniform," supposedly expressing spontaneity and freedom, at first dismay us. But remember that expression, to have meaning, demands an appropriate audience. All expression in symbols is social. Inevitably, both the Establishment and the disaffected must depend for their internal solidarities upon communication, which requires mutual comprehension and credibility. Real expression of individuality unfortunately implies a certain similarity among individuals.

Few exotic elements enter into daily life merely as unsought intrusions of the unfamiliar; most novelty is deliberately introduced by someone. Individuals universally borrow substance for their own perceived identities from outside, so exotic representations really make up much of personal display. Schooling, at all levels of a modern society, outfits individuals with bits of knowledge and skill from the outside or the past, which they may use to demonstrate their worth. Some thereupon even employ their symbolism in a negative sense, becoming juvenile heroes or he-men by rejecting such book learning or fine manners. Office girls vie with each other in recounting the details of incidents portrayed on television the night before; more pretentious people smother conversation at parties by regurgitating verbatim the content of the newsmagazines. Women's fashions classically exemplify the principle that strangeness from afar confers distinction, and that those who brandish it remain invulnerable to both ridicule and physical discomfort.

It would seem that cultural change generally, and accordingly also the economic development process, would depend very largely upon the incorporation of exotic innovation into individual display behavior. Someone has to choose and foster novelty. Traditional elites attached to an older social order and technical system not infrequently face challenges from younger, underprivileged persons whose only hope for real advancement lies in riding into power on a wave of innovation. Students of social and political revolution have often remarked on the social marginality of major exponents of new ideas. In many countries the birthplace of most of the political leaders, for instance, is geographically "marginal," i.e., peripheral, to the national core zone. When established vehicles of self-expression and advancement are denied to them, men will grasp for new ones. Supposing all available means of self-proclamation and enhancement, whatever their nature and source, to be repartitioned throughout the membership of a community, then the exotic elements must fall to someone, and he perhaps becomes the advocate of change. Such a situation, modified by social differences, may well explain the progress of the diffusion of cultural elements. Not only individuals but also institutions may involve themselves therein. In fact, considered from a certain standpoint, institutions amount to nothing other than devices for effectuating change, by advancing certain groups and persons and by implanting new ideas. The cellular structure of societies divided into institutional units enables them to adjust more finely and responsively to changing external connections and internal conditions.

The Dialectic of Expression

Settlements as displays, representing all their past and present denizens through individual material creations, and manifesting their corporate identity, their customs, rules, and rhythms in the concrete features of their landscapes, form a central subject of study for cultural geography. No complete catalog of their features, needless to say, has ever been made or ever can be, for each place stands apart as unique and particular. Nonetheless, the particulars group into general types, and the movements of change can be traced geographically. A morphology of settlements brings out inevitable resemblances and regularities, so that regional distributions and relationships appear. Field patterns, agricultural practices, house types, internal circulation and zonation, industrial processes, decorative motifs, all reveal a larger geographic order. Moreover, the historical progress of innovations, as they move through communication channels and expressive landscape, lends itself to accurate summation. Thereby, geographers invoke both the concept of the "cultural landscape" and the notion of "culture history" in explanation, and cast their findings in the framework of "culture areas." The genesis of culture areas, however, results from dynamic processes not always clearly indexed by resulting forms, or accounted for by known connections. Hence, in order to provide an adequate account of culture areas, their formative processes—which again fall into general types—may need consideration. The investigations of "cultural ecology" attend to this need.

Communication processes complete themselves through expression in environments, but that expression emerges, at last, only out of work. An idea takes material shape in the world only when translated into an object or a sensible attribute of an object. Art illustrates this principle: the artist wrestles with his material in order to compel it to express his vision. Recalcitrant words or stones or harmonies have to be subdued by dogged work. A real artist reveals his integrity in this stubborn effort, refusing to compromise his master vision to accommodate the material, forcing it insistently to yield and take the shape he dictates. That is what the world admires in artists—they struggle with nature, whereas others, like engineers, settle for compromise. No wonder art communicates as nothing else can!

The point here is that all communication rests upon some kind of interaction with the environment. And all expressive style and form is as if wrenched from nature, the fruit of struggle. The ways of making nature yield to mankind's expressive urge are many, and unanimously difficult. And so every landscape, every settlement embodies the result of long and tense relations of the people with the environment, the marks of slowly-growing skill and potency, and slowly-crystallizing certainties of form. Distinctive and harmonious expression gradually unfolds. Ideas conscripted everywhere impinge upon the process, and are sorted and recast, rejected or adapted into concrete guises. A dialectical encounter develops between imported cultural ideas and the local forces of nature, remaking both. The communication that flows from area to area among humanity enters into another sort of exchange between surrounding nature and the man at work. All undergoes translations and reformulations. Just as Shakespeare, when translated into German or Russian, reputedly becomes something else if equally as great, ideas translated into landscape metamorphose.

Utter uniformity is seldom. Some environments accept what others reject or suppress. Communication, incorporeal and potential, distilling experience into stimuli for action, leads not to perfect likeness but to partial differentiation. Secret shapes emerging in expression instigate diverse behavior. Culture, the learned and taught, insinuates itself pliably into environment. How? That is the next question.

CHAPTER **5** *environmental*

learning

Communication shapes the individual. Heredity, social intercourse, and experimentation—all legitimate facets of communication in the widest sense—together with multifarious accidental influences, make men what they are. Genetic propensities presumably come to the surface as individuals grow. The genetically inherited element in individual character and behavior may considerably exceed what once was guessed at, but it is by definition conveyed outside the play of normal environmental influences.

Human migrations, distributing genetic strains, may well play a part in determining not merely anatomical details of different populations, but deeper physiology and latent capacities and aptitudes as well. Their geographical significance would relate, not to a total superiority or inferiority of different human stocks, but to more or less efficient adaptation to particular climatic and other natural conditions—and thus to numerous immiscible "superiorities" of physical adaptation proper to specific environments. Altogether too little knowledge now exists of any such differences to permit acceptable generalizations, however. The abiding hostility of geographers to theories of human bio-adaptation has precluded their studying this theme. At the level of the individual, nevertheless, everyone will readily recognize genetic differences among families that declare themselves in physical build, strength, and longevity. Out of the genetic inheritance, life and experience elicit strong expressions of some characteristics and slighter ones of others. Genetics does not make the man (as clothes allegedly do), but it helps.

Apart from inheritance, accidental exposures to the whims of nature and the chances of life, registered perceptually, play their own considerable role in forming persons. This theme has always been a major one in drama and the novel. "Fate" fascinates and frightens us. Indeed, people commonly use the actually neutral word "accident" to imply something dangerous or deadly. But fatalities and injuries aside, accident affects a person's development in accordance with his perception of it or reaction to it—that is, as he integrates it into the rest of his experience. Unsystematic interferences in systems, unpredictable and meaningless events, perturb our lives. As a formative element, accident functions through reactions that arise from previous development, and so only insofar as perception masters it and accommodates it to continuing experience. Unless interpreted as a feature of an *orderly* environment, accident remains inscrutable and irrelevant to life.

Human intercourse and man's experimental insight into nature are transactional; they bring together order with order to generate another order dialectically. Together, often alternating ideas and action, the two transactions teach. Learning, the more or less permanent acquisition of new behaviors, results from them. What happens changes both the world and man. Culture implies both teaching and learning, otherwise it would not contribute to man's continuity. Within culture, expressiveness has its counterpoise in learning through environment.

The process of learning, subject of much disputation, reduces to a series of transactions. Without doing violence to delicate theoretical issues, we may legitimately say that it involves first the presentation of a stimulus by environment, i.e., through direct person-to-person intercourse or expressive artifacts. Learning begins when the individual reacts observantly. The exposure leads next to a test: the learner submits his response to empirical validation, experimenting in natural and social spheres. He may try out his skill at executing some motion and watch the result, repeating the exercise and readjusting his stance and movements until he masters it. That is how a boy learns to climb a tree or throw a ball. Feedback shapes succeeding attempts to perfect the maneuver. Something analogous occurs when learning to pronounce a foreign language; the student feels for the unfamiliar tensions in throat and tongue. A watchful teacher helps him. Coaching, by comment and example, aids mastery. The social context demands testing other persons' critical reactions, over and above mastering the skills themselves. Having at last achieved control of a maneuver and having adjusted it to social expectations, a person then still has to fit it into his own life and activity pattern.

Assuming a need for certain basic activity to ensure survival, human beings, in the course of keeping alive, have to learn. Inertia and unresponsiveness would be deadly. What they learn may be minimal, no doubt, and much of it asocial. The learning indispensable for infant and child survival, however, rests as much, if not more, on transactions of a social sort as on those between the individual and his inanimate environment. A man's very existence in nature imposes activity; society, equally imperious, requires involvement. In other words, a child may need no internal "motivation" to learn; his environment pushes him to it in spite of himself. Making good and faithful use of what has been learned is quite another matter.

Places of Learning

Consider an example. A school represents the dominant social system. As an institution it concerns itself, even more than most institutions, with disseminating information. Yet it has difficulty in imparting the aspects of the general culture it attempts to transmit. Analyzed in terms of *environmental* learning, as here conceived, the modern North American school reveals serious shortcomings. The environment intended to express desired concepts and models competes very poorly, at most age levels, with rival attractions. The teacher and her lesson are less arresting spectacles than squirming, smirking schoolmates. The schoolwork, maps, and pictures posted round the classroom cannot compare in fascination with whatever may go on outside the windows. The instituted rhythms lull alertness away. Moreover, the schoolroom even under the best conditions cannot engage all pupils simultaneously in a good experimental context, in which they find out for themselves what they really want to know, and discover how to master things. School, as all of us remember it, was mostly waiting. A single child can so eagerly absorb one or more adults' full attention that for the teachers to keep up with a whole classroom is hopeless. Children in roomload lots may be placated and neutralized, but not absorbed in dialogue. No ordinary school environment allows all the children to grow by their own testing, all at once, all day. And finally, the school environment is totally unreal. How can a child believe that what he finds there will apply to life? Even the language deviates from what companions, parents, and the television speak, and hence can hardly fail to signal something foreign and irrelevant. The schoolroom truce and its daylight curfew, so utterly unlike the child's explosive, labile version of a world, repels enthusiasm and vitality, and represents no future that he wants to live in. No matter if this arraignment exaggerates somewhat; its substance holds.

North American elementary schools, of course, epitomize a great profusion of different institutions, everywhere implicated in the learning process, and surely are no worse than most of these others. Some traditional schools, notably the old Chinese or koranic kind where learning went by rote, may nonetheless have made more sense than is commonly assumed—if not more sense than Western schools. For the mandarin or cadi, as the schoolboys knew from personal experience, would by profession intone or expound the classics all their lives, in the same way that they had learned in school; such schools befitted the settings. Rote learning fits in places where a verbal ritual survives. Be that as it may, the major point in this discussion is the relative clumsiness of institutions in managing the initial, basic learning processes, despite their normal role in disseminating information. Judging by the obvious success of some religious institutions in managing and containing learning, and considering their methods, one might fairly suppose that the formal institution's job is to isolate and shield the novice from an impure and turbulent world. A school perhaps at best curtails insidious involvements, at least for hours at a time.

Informal, spontaneous relationships and influences, associated circumstantially with formal schools and monasteries, may guide learning more than the latter. Currently the fear haunts North America that student "counterculture" may prevail in school and colleges, instilling loyalties and habits that the older generation abhors and dreads. Perhaps the boring, passive, unreal quality accused in many schoolrooms plays a role in this. The issue is not power, only information. Within institutions, even the powerless may operate defiant networks of communication. Prisoners do so everywhere, and furthermore, as is well known, they do their best thereby to advance the criminal training of the young among them. Formal institutions, then, as well as informal, may become involved in the learning process, and a dialectic tension and dissonance may arise between the two types. Undoubtedly the institutions most concerned, notably various kinds of face to face groups, suffer little from the dissonance because of their smaller compass.

The real geography of learning centers on the home. Parents and close family members, with a few exceptions, exercise the dominant influence during the early years of life. And that is the time of a child's voracious and voluminous learning. Peer groups, too, begin early to exert a major effect, starting with the siblings who are most children's constant company, and going on to their age mates at school, at work, and in like situations. The circle expands modestly from household to village circumference, and may either widen to cover a rather larger, familiar locality, compact in form and lifelong intimately known, or metamorphose into a kind of web of spotty locations linked by long journeys. In the face to face, peer-dominated universe, a person continues to learn during most of his life from his fellows. As means of independent learning, artifacts (e.g., books) provide alternatives. Yet only in recent times have certain media like the television put the child into such frequent and close confrontation with utter strangers as to threaten to outweigh the family and peers as factors in his learning. Bookish children always did exist, to the mixed consternation and delight of their parents, but in some countries now almost every child is a "Box baby"—with uncertain implications. No one really knows what part television has played, through weaning children early from their families' influence, in creating an alleged "generation gap." However, there can be little doubt that a new environment of learning now exists, and that it can produce some radical results.

Whatever its contexts, learning must proceed by trial and error within them. As modern schools can hardly suffice for the experimental phase of learning, so television and related media suffer the defect of a one-way quality that prevents their functioning as complete teaching devices. Necessarily lacking playback, they only distribute unconfirmed, if often convincing, representations. Their immense capability for falsehood is notably ill-concealed, but still insidious. The advent of these media may conceivably have introduced an age of fatal illusionism. As their domain proceeds—if indeed it does so—to engird the earth, a decision on this point is bound to be forthcoming, for nature's forces relentlessly subject ideas to trial, and punish error mercilessly.

Environmental Selection

"Trial and error," from the human standpoint, describes the learning process; from the standpoint of nature, learning amounts to a process of eliminating unsuccessful modifications. Natural selection, albeit a relatively permissive natural selection, emphatically governs human behavior. We allude to "social evolution" and "regional development" as such rather than to the disasters and failures that, by and large, have determined their courses. As individuals learn the limits of their own possibilities through making mistakes, societies discover their directions through costly blundering and squandering. No view of mankind as the purposeful, enlightened steward of the earth can stand up to the overwhelming evidence of ignorance and clumsiness as mainstays of man's tenancy. The illusion may well rest, however, on the fact that individuals can capriciously set in motion vicious processes, yet seldom pay for them themselves. Even whole societies can instigate disaster and escape scot-free. But mankind in the end must pay. Selection operates, accordingly, at almost imperceptible levels. Society, pliable, readjusts and absorbs; the cost of mistakes is apportioned in miniscule levies on everyone; effects become lost in a welter of shifting careers. But environment exacts respect. Over time, the penalties for error can compound, enough to enervate a people. The costs accumulate and come to weigh oppressively on society. Opulence, through carelessness, gives way to penury.

Natural selection, screening out relentlessly the minor imperfections that random recombination of the genes induces among organisms, forces the long-term development of any species by slight steps down a certain path, as if it were preordained. As a result, under the pressure of different environments and special roles within those environments, the several different lines of descent diverge, until distinct new species have appeared. (The process recalls dialect formation.) Logically, the case of local social groups, searching out successful ways of life, should be little different. By small increments, environmental penalties and rewards should tell in social evolution. Trial and error constitutes the core of learning by experiment, and in effect consists of no more than environmental screening. Concrete costs and gains, but also promises and warnings sensed by man, inevitably must shape behavior. The quiet operation of such environmental controls upon societies, so thoroughly obscure, conceals this obvious relationship within. Clear proofs cannot be adduced for "environmental adjustment" in general. Yet logically, any settlement that lasts must do so at the sufferance of nature, and with the concurrence of the larger society in which it is implicated.

Nowhere better than in crop plants and barnyard animals does the joint effect of natural and social screening show. Infinitesimal changes taking place each generation add up to current cultigens. The process of domestication suggests a sort of endless game of chess between human beings and nature, each move leading to a countermove, but all together leading to a changed situation on the board. Watchful trial and error brought about the transformation of wild plants, some of them surely less than prepossessing, into ample and reliable producers. The epic of experiment that lies behind the crop plants left almost no record until some real success had been secured by man. Unmodified wild plants (or undetectably altered ones), nonetheless, do gradually give way, according to the archaeological record, to recognizably domesticated ones. How many mistakes it took to get that far cannot be known, but the fact is, notably, that only in a few places did this dialectical development go far enough that well-identified, distinctive genetic lines became established. Although the actual process of domestication by trial and error must have gotten under way as soon as man was man, with the necessary alertness and foresight to carry it along, enduring achievements from the experiments likely to have happened universally apparently came out of a few concentrated zones. Only here and there, with great good luck, were some domesticators able to lay a firm enough foundation so that at some point their living creations stabilized and success began to pile up on success. Then their achievement snowballed, perhaps drawing in contributions from neighbors, and ennobling a goodly element of the potentially useful wild plants of their region. This kind of evolution has distinguished about a half dozen areas in all the world. The acknowledged centers or "hearths" of domestication—which embrace animals as well as plants—attest to rare combinations of insight, persistence, and luck on the part of a few communities.

Thus the wealth of the Indies lay in the taro, banana, sugar cane, citrus, ginger, and rice that seem to have developed in an area east of Bengal and south of the Yangtze. With them can be listed fowl, and perhaps pig and duck. To do full justice to the achievement of this center, the lists of plants recreated would have to run into the hundreds, including an impressive variety not only of familiar foods, but also exotic spices, unfamiliar vegetables and fruits, medicinal plants, textile and dye species, and yet others. Moreover, a staggering assortment of traditional garden ornamentals, distinctive to the same area and of uneven antiquity, would beg to be added. The accretion of new members to the great company of plants which developed in very early times (before 2000 B.C.), has expanded the lot. Numerous borrowings from other areas, as well as the initial local domestic stocks, have ramified under the hand of Oriental gardeners into a profusion of distinct varieties, each catering to some particular demand and taste, or adjusting delicately to a certain soil or climate. The corollary of all this variation, of course, is the equally striking differentiation of human communities and their life-ways, directly linked with crops and climate.

The domesticated treasure of Asia has been shared in later days with other peoples elsewhere, after having permeated nearby regions. Some crops traveled worldwide, fitting in wherever climate and culture permitted. So it has been with the orange, sugar, and rice, advancing through Arabia on to America. New varieties have meanwhile, and consequently, continued to proliferate. Additional techniques of cultivation have also arisen in due time, reflecting inexhausted adaptability in the crops. The diffusion, or more accurately the dissemination or dispersal, of the respective plants and animals has followed institutional channels, and their further genetic radiations and new cultivation practices conform to normal processes of spatial differentiation.

In discussing the dissemination of something like a crop, which carries with it both implications of utility and ethnic and aesthetic overtones, we stumble on a puzzling and redoubtable problem in geographical dynamics. Why do people accept or reject a given innovation? Leaving underlying preference and motive to psychologists, the geographer may nonetheless take heed of expressive qualities affecting such transactions. Potential recipients may well differ in ability to read a use implied in form, depending on their previous experience; peoples unfamiliar with cultivation of field grains may not have been so hospitable to rice, at first, as seedfarmers. Lacking a tradition of preparing textiles from a certain sort of fiber plant in special ways, undoubtedly some neighbors of the Eastern domesticators, for example, did not borrow jute or ramie. It must have taken a rare imagination at first, too, to see the value in mulberry and silkworm.

Associations of prestige and delight likewise count. Perhaps local concepts of beauty affect acceptance of a plant even as a crop. One such factor is color. In Central America, certain brilliant red and yellow amaranths, whose ancestral role was agricultural, are now grown for ornament. The expressive values of this sort that might encourage the adoption of new plants and animals, it seems, apply again in the retention of old crops or animals whose usefulness has ended or diminished.

The nearly antieconomic horse is doing very well again in North America; the number of horses currently occupied in providing pleasure and amusement may even surpass the highest total ever attained by draft- and plowhorses on this continent. A great many ornamental garden plants, to say nothing of weeds, can count an episode of usefulness in their history. They have survived because of other attractions. If such retentions and readaptations are understandable, then so perhaps is borrowing with like inducements.

The relation of a foreign plant or animal to personal display is easy to imagine; even now gardeners avidly seek new exotic varieties of fuchsias, begonias, primulas, or roses to which to append their name and fame. Generations of intrepid plant seekers have enriched the gardens, hothouses, orchards, and fields of Europe and America with both wild and domestic plants from afar. Perhaps the exploits of the great Soviet plant hunt of the 1920's and 1930's stand out most. The Russians thoroughly canvassed the world's useful plants. Their lists substantiate the notion of a few major hearths of domestication.

As earlier suggested, individual display avails itself of opportunities encountered, and someone always welcomes the exotic and the rare new find. The spread of improved plants should constitute nothing exceptional, and its motivation ought to correspond to widespread human inclination. Here, though, we can witness how expressive attributes may enter into cultural dispersals.

Another side to these same dispersals, of course, belongs to ecology. Domestic plants and animals can spread if and only if environments welcome them. Hence any transplantation of a crop not only evokes practical considerations and expressive qualities, but also requires definite environmental similarities between the new home and the old. Only in favorable locations can genetic adaptation then proceed to operate. A fine example of this principle relates to the exchange of plants between Europe and America, subsequent upon discovery and conquest. Around 1500, Europe planted crops that mostly had originated in the Middle Eastern center of domestication. Barley, wheat, rye, and oats (the latter two replacing wheat in more severe conditions), augmented by a sizeable amount of millet and by buckwheat, provided the basic staple for gruel or bread. Cabbages, onions, carrots, and turnips dominated among vegetables. Fibers from hemp and flax, as well as wool and animal skins, went into clothing. Spices were costly and few, since imported; sugar, citrus fruits, bananas, and other products known to the Arabs did not penetrate further north; silk and cotton, both exotic, vied in rarity and costliness. Horse, cow, sheep, goat, and pig accompanied the plants.

The agriculture of Aztec Mexico, of course, utterly differed from Europe's. The Indians, gardeners rather than plowmen, centered their effort on corn (maize), along with squashes, chilies, and beans, but lesser crops were abundant. Cotton and agave fibers were spun for clothing and textiles. Further south in the Andes, a complex of crops focusing on and epitomized by the potato had developed, bearing only modest resemblances to Mexico's.

When the culture worlds collided, the Europeans initially attempted to introduce their own crops. Wheat failed in the tropical lowlands, and only later took hold at high altitudes. The foreign crops mostly proved altogether unsuited to American conditions. But one contingent, coming by way of the Arabs and subtropical Spain from the Orient, found itself very much at home, so that sugar, especially, became exceedingly important in the later colonial developments. In the subsequent century, tropical crops flooded into America both by the Spanish route and directly from Asia by way of the Philippines, or from Africa to Brazil. On the other hand, the major American crops, at home mainly in highland areas, tended to accommodate well to the cool European climates. The Mediterranean countries appear to have received the first wave from America—maize, tomato, chili, squashes—which somehow eddied and settled eastwardly, leaving the Turkish Empire endowed with a host of new crops. Only later did the stream trickle northward and again westward. Hence countries like Georgia, the plains of Serbia, Wallachia, Moldavia, Ukraine, and Anatolia itself—all provinces or borderlands of Turkey at the time—accepted maize as a staple, which it continues to be. The Hungarians seized upon the chili and out of it created their beloved paprika. Italy and the Levant welcomed the tomato, which revolutionized their cookery. Meanwhile and for long after, northern and western Europe continued to subsist on gruels and cabbages, permitting itself no more than light flirtations with the new exotic crops. Only the potato finally secured a place, and that but slowly, for it had to inch its way from Britain eastward into Prussia, Poland, and Russia, and across to Ireland.

The dispersal of the plants described, expressed in one stream from highland Mexico over into Turkey and thence northward, another from Peru to northwest and northeast Europe, and others out of Asia and Africa by various routes, conformed both to expressive attributes of the plants concerned and to ecological requirements. In regard to the former, the prevalent early interest in New World plants as curiosities and decorations was noteworthy. Many of the Indian crops first turned up in curio gardens, and some, like the tomato, long continued more to entertain than to nourish northern Europeans. The record would remain incomplete without allusion, incidentally, to that sinful gift, tobacco, which enjoyed a special easy triumph among Europeans, Orientals, and whoever met it; it moved around the world alone, ahead of empires. Prestige and pleasure counted.

A lot of learning must accompany acceptance of a crop. One consequence of any dispersal may well be the spread of entire complexes of associations and activities connected with it. In order to grow maize, the farmer needs to master practices for dealing with it, and the household has to grow accustomed to the cob, the large grains, the husks, and must make places for them in diet and in craft. Cornstalks and cornhusks, serving many rustic uses, are as thoroughly at home in the Balkans as the foodstuff corn. A modification of diet inevitably follows upon new introductions, and one is tempted to inquire to what extent cuisine itself reflects techniques and tastes transmitted with the crop. How much does the Hungarian cuisine owe to the Mexican, whence its chili came? Do South American Indian cooking practices with manioc recur among the Africans and Indonesians who grow the borrowed crop? No doubt such influences do not carry far; it would appear, in fact, that only when favorable expressive features can come into play will larger complexes—always with the exception of purely technical necessity—remain intact.

Complex Dispersals

For the purpose of assessing the likelihood of more complex dispersals, architecture offers good material. Within the sphere of building, two complementary, sometimes interfusing tendencies prevail. Master architects and anonymous builders work parallel. The latter, on the whole, receive and pass along traditions, modifying them to suit the individual circumstances of the job and the user's desire. Probably the chain of connections responsible for architectural details of anonymous or vernacular buildings resembles that which binds together introductions of a crop in different places, that is, it tends to be hand-to-hand, fragmented, accidental and irregular. No overall purpose informs it. That is not to say, of course, that vernacular architecture responds to no consistencies. In fact the builder trains apprentices and exercises an influence on his congeners within the guild. The precedent furnished by local examples of finished constructions must in addition enforce or inspire some consistency. But significant combinations of particular features, especially excessively idiosyncratic and difficult ones, betray most commonly the hand of one master and his disciples. For everyday, unknown carpenters, practicality almost rules them out. At most they may afford a few flourishes, but no lavish display of invention and virtuosity. Furthermore, anonymous architecture remains exceedingly tied to locality; cantonment is diagnostic even of its finer fantasies, whereas the "public" architect will disperse his characteristic style far and wide.

The ordinary house exemplifies the vernacular. House form, contriving a delicate local adjustment among sites, materials, and traditions, evolves toward distinctiveness accordingly. The houses even of North America, despite the aesthetic profligacy and material prodigality peculiar to new countries, accord not badly with regional divisions. The older and poorer forms, to be sure, differ most. Along the Connecticut River, placards on homes reveal the date of building (increasingly late northward) and afford an insight into gradually proceeding adaptation to the locale. The local version of the New England frame cottage—and also the distinctive white wooden churches—preserve clear marks of heritage and habitat. They contrast markedly with Virginia's sprawling country houses, comparatively much vaster, and their clusters of what once were slave quarters and worksheds. The brick townhouses and public halls, and even brick city streets of larger eastern ports, preserve another adaptation. Quebec furnishes the example of yet a different cultural tradition ensconced in a harsher setting, with its compact stone or wooden cottages. In contrast to all these, a great sea of roughly mid-nineteenth century Gothic houses, gaunt and taciturn as Grant Wood's people, inundates the Midwest. In the hills and woods of the Deep South, other odd forms like the "dogtrot" double cabin have survived. Continuing to ramble over the continent, we can encounter double-doored cabins in the Ozarks, adobe in the Southwest, a surprising abundance of log houses still used in the Mountain States, and, in early Pacific Coastal shipping villages, New England houses again, here touched strongly with Gothic. If dwellings of the Indians come into account, of course, a great many more forms may survive at least vestigially: longhouse, teepee, Pueblo cluster, hogan, pit-house, *ramada,* Northwest plank-house.

The vernacular housetypes enumerated, and others similar, evolved in context and in use. From them, architects have occasionally taken their motifs, and some of them, e.g., the Gothic farmhouse, did have architects among their "ancestors." North American towns and cities are replete with examples of all the vernacular types, modified for urban use and taste. Hardly a house form has been invented in America that does not occur, in imitation, in Chicago, Los Angeles, and Seattle. Not only that: a giddy wealth of Aztec, Andalusian, Punjabi, Norman, Egyptian, Swiss, Chinese, Kentish, Moorish, and other exotica decorates the residential streets. The profusion of pastiche perhaps has no counterpart anywhere else in architecture. True vernacular houses, however, exhibit a spareness and sincerity befitting the conditions they accommodate. Little superfluous or irrelevant ornament obstructs their clear image. Herein, they contrast with the "great" architecture of most periods, in which personal display, on the part of the artist and on behalf of the patron, runs riot. The truly great, as distinguished from the fashionable and successful alone, create unities of design, the mark of all real art; the rest collect details. The great architecture of the world impresses its bold profiles and its individual completenesses on beholders. The ornament, no matter how rich, submits to the wholeness harmoniously. The starkness of the Egyptian pyramids, Machu Picchu in Peru, Stonehenge, or the antique wooden temples of Japan is not more entire than the perfect concert of detail in the great cathedrals, the mosques of the Registan in Samarkand, or Angkor Wat. In fact, many older monuments now bereft of decoration and fine detail, like Mexican and Greek temples,

73

were once richly painted and ornamented. The wealth of expression in such buildings conveys the genius of the architects in its own immediate manner, and uniquely. This sort of expression characteristically recurs in any building a master creates and, what is also notable, in the works of his disciples and pupils to a varying degree.

The whole history of Gothic architecture in Europe, for example, forms a unity, and its course can be followed explicitly in the activities, travels, and teaching of a handful of men, sponsored in turn by a few prelates and potentates. Stemming from one project in the twelfth-century Île-de-France, under the patronage of the abbot of St. Denis, the style, a most elaborate concretion of motifs and details, and an embodiment of radical new principles of construction, spread by way of the actual commissions of one architect, and later of his apprentices, throughout an area reaching as far as England, Portugal and Spain, Sicily, Hungary, Bohemia, and Sweden, and of course centered on France. Authentic Gothic, built during the succeeding two centuries or so, and somewhat diverging into national schools, occurs in all this great area. The style, a particularly apt expression not only of the architect's genius, but also both of the abbot's and his king's lofty aspirations and of the symbolism of the medieval church, presents a clear case of an entire articulated complex of ideas, a cultural whole, which spread nearly integrally. It virtually coincided in its time with Roman Christendom. The dispersal of so grand and vast a system calls for infinitely more than a "diffusion" of ideas, or even a process dominated by a central force. It involves painstaking adherence to an exacting pattern wherever the system spreads, the mastery of endless fine points of expression and engineering, and still the presentation of a single whole. Masterworks of architecture can command our awe in part because of such demands upon their builders, and the very idea of such cultural integrity in motion, too, compels respect.

An almost endless list of such geographies of architectural styles could be compiled to testify to how culture complexes may spread. Even restricting such a list to what we now regard as buildings, and only taking into account the ones still standing in a good state of preservation, what hundreds of traditions, and thousands of variants, are known! It would take many lifetimes to visit them all even hastily. Each of these many traditions in architecture combines technical and artistic apprenticeship with central power and with established channels of communication to produce singularly eloquent expressions of the builders in their particular environmental frames.

Then think of cities. Insofar as a city conforms to a style and expresses tradition and power, it can indicate the same things. The Chinese urban system, wherever it becomes established, most emphatically carries on its patterns. At the zenith of their power, the Moslems, too, disseminated their kind of city along with their architecture, both of which had multiple roots in lands they annexed. The so-called modern industrial city preserves consistency everywhere it goes, and it goes everywhere. Infinite apprenticeships, uncountable hierarchies of minor power, and a babble of half-reconciled expressions mark this latest unitary cultural expansion. The modern city, and the succession of architectural styles within it, recur faithfully amid the most diverse surroundings, juxtaposed with enormously contrasting natural domains. But the universal technology that constructs and operates them, and the universal commerce that pumps life through them, keep them uniform.

To return to older monuments, harking back to even earlier, less well-recorded periods, substantial evidence of moving culture complexes remains in odd and widespread earthworks. Almost every country proves upon investigation to abound with ancient burial mounds, fortifications, ceremonial platforms, waterworks, causeways, terraced fields, defensive walls, and other massive constructions built by peoples lost to history. The sparsely-chronicled "Scythians," for instance, scattered underground tombs over the steppe; one hardly knows the people's origin or real identity. Most primeval builders, such as the authors of Stonehenge and Avebury or of the endless terraces of Peru, remain unidentified. Therein lies a vast and vague tale, and therefrom stems a whole geography of silent witnesses. They merge ultimately into recognizable tombs, temples, cultivated areas, and settlements. So numerous and nearly ubiquitous are such odd monuments that their geography has still to be recounted, and new discoveries of startling scope continue to occur.

The dispersal of crops epitomizes a sort of export of experience, most sensitive, in turn, to new experience. Their origins rooted in particular dialectics that fit them only for a given place, domestic plants and animals must undergo reintegration through evolutionary change whenever they move into a new setting. As the organism changes, so must the land to receive it and so must its growers. Unlike the instance of master architectural style, which disperses intact under the multiple guidance of teaching and authority to insert itself imperiously into any setting, the perhaps equally complex entities that make up cropping systems manifest a nearly servile suppleness in adaptation. In the case of architecture, the necessities of artistic style, of sacred or secular signification, and of power's vanity importunately dictate the outcome, not seldom overriding nature (e.g., the siting of Saint Petersburg-Leningrad in a cold swamp!) as well as local ways of life. The grander monumental complexes disdain concessions to circumstance, partaking thereby of the distinguishing freedom of art. On the other hand, the very intricacy of crop systems expresses an almost limitless acquiescence to small necessities of environment, and enlists the cultivators themselves in an exacting conformity. Both rest on learning, the former holding ever-loyal to models and ideals internalized, the other bending pliantly to all external pressures and therein, learning to survive. There is a kind of learning that, once mastered, steadfastly defies and conquers circumstances, and another kind that, always forming, yields to live.

Art in Environment

The two extremes of our ecology, the "spirit" and the "world," are dual dwelling places of mankind. Both manifest themselves in action, both register within environments. Each draws upon the other for its rationale, so that the animal pursuit of livelihood becomes in man transfigured into something with a style and message. Display of selfhood redirects the self toward eternity. The spirit clothes itself in turn in earthly forms, infusing its own principles into created things. Man's spiritual world is materialized, his material world spiritualized. Yet their congruence remains precarious and even dubious. Behind an imaginary value-laden nature man suspects a cold indifference to himself and all his dreams. Art, finding its freedom in perfecting the material, has to manufacture value for us. But nature does not follow art, alas, and even science—that most curious of arts!—steers between delusion and futility, since nothing guarantees that logical and mathematical order has anything at all to do with nature, or with life. And art still bravely, grandly conjures for us. It creates from nothing full, entire environments—their unity the measure of perfection—within environment, empaneling a world of value in them by revealing forms selected and arranged according to sublime intuitions of order. Through such integral, alternative existences, apart from time, deferring to no mean expediencies, man experiences himself in new dimensions.

Expression in art of the deepest, most fundamental aspects of life in any civilization is acknowledged. The validity of its statements rests upon the artist's insight into his time and its ways, and equally upon his faithfulness to his vision and his mastery of means for exposing it. Inevitably there arises a question as to the possibility of knowing the spirit of a culture, of a time, through its art. Can we read, for instance, the underlying premises and emphases of Babylonian civilization in the bas-reliefs of ruined palaces, the cuneiform epics and poems, the carvings on the cylinder-seals? A certain cruel solidity seems to shine through them. Similarly, do not the painting, poetry, music, and sculpture of Europe between 1900 and 1950 betray an analytic, inorganic outlook, touched with anomie? If artists are true in their vision and loyal to it, their interpretations of their cultures must be peerless and indispensable.

Consequently, a geography of art, not as a catalog of techniques or dry compendium of names and dates, but as a comprehensive map of meanings, suggests itself. This geography accords and blends with that of architecture, for religious and funerary buildings, especially, incorporate all manner of great art, and when still frequented by the devotees of their cults, certainly could exhibit even more of chant and incense, poetry and choruses, juggling and processions, candles and flowers. In order to sense the place of the arts in the reverential-festive atmosphere of religion, one has only to imagine mass in a Spanish church, with its paintings, gilt altars, singing, vestment, lights, and pageantry; or witness the display in Oriental temples, rich in forms and sounds and colors. Only cultures without faith would bother with museums. Objectified, art pales. Architecture, music, literature, sculpture, painting, dance—and arts more localized as well—conform somehow to common influences, and hence, we suppose, afford a multilateral but essentially unanimous rendition of the spirit of a culture in a given phase. With them go the minor handicrafts and humdrum products of the period, to whatever degree the social divisions among their makers may permit and encourage such unanimity. Peasant art tends not to dovetail with the gentlefolk's for it marches to another music. Themes and treatments slowly percolating down from lofty origins declare themselves in later peasant derivations; thus it is with legends, tunes, prayers, costume, dances. Some peasant communities tenaciously retain the ancient decorative motifs (e.g., inner Eurasian floral designs that still flourish in both Finnish and Balkan embroidery and house decoration) and slyly ape the manners of the long-gone court. Hence this geography of art has divers depths.

To collect and compare examples of the art of different peoples, trying perhaps to discern its deeper implications, differs altogether from acquiring through one's own familiar orbit meaning revealed and reiterated in its native art. Within the environments of learning art becomes a crucial element. The sense of life can only be imparted, according to the given dispensation, through devices that transcend the commonplace and literal. All the subliminal and implicit communication that transpires face to face employs such devices. Art, however, says things that people cannot tell each other even without words—it is the voice not of a person but of a world.

Probably, then, even the homely ornamentation that a technically simple folk apply, such as the painted pebbles and the rhythmic lines scratched into bone from the end of the Paleolithic era, convey something important. It is unclear if there exists some people absolutely without art, lacking even body decoration. Beyond art as such, there is all the discipline of gesture, working-motions, the collective dancelike evolutions of crowds, or games. The ways are learned. And subsequently, all those ineffable lessons cannot but express themselves in forms, into what the bodily motions themselves become, as if frozen there forever, when men create. Things made are motion's fossils. The subsidiary geography of such involuntary artlike expression, too, deserves attention. Whence come the strange, persistent differences between the overwhelmingly curvilinear and the largely rectilinear traditions that repeatedly contrast in Asia, Africa, and America? Why are some people given to crowded design and others to spare? (Compare later China with Japan.) What governs the contrast between the bold and the pale colors used in design by different peoples? These are questions to ponder. No doubt, all such modalities of expression belong to culture, descending from generation to generation as inherited significances intelligible to a people and reproduced by them onward through time, long persisting.

In contrast, fashion, which also constitutes a universe of authenticity and integrity like art, lives by change. Even so-called primitive art bears witness on occasion to a sweep of new fashions, and modern art abounds in rapidly succeeding schools. Fashion in the sense of changing ideals of form—and prescinding from its role in individual competitive display—may perhaps at times herald any more extensive social change. The geographical career of fashions seems capricious. Its volatile existence is like all of cultural dissemination, only as if parodied or sketched. For fashion also has its own authorities—at odds, most often, with the grave established ones—its pathways, and its adaptations.

Architecture and art generally, and all sorts of design, evidently communicate and teach. But learning from them must be different from learning by trial and error. Expression meets perception, yes; but where is the experimentation that confirms? The forms of art are not for imitation or for testing. What the poem or the music tells, although made patent in its forms, and immediate to sense, does not translate itself—it transforms the perceiver. The test of art is living, feeling. Something like recognition, followed by clarity and alertness—that is the process of beholding. Learning from art and design is a special learning, and although all their expressions occur in environment, not all the process is truly "environmental."

The previous chapter dealt with environmental expression; the present one concerns environmental perception. The two topics not only complement each other; they are facets of the same transaction. "Perception," now a fashionable word among geographers, refers to and includes more than learning; it embraces the untested and untestable, the irrelevant and unassimilable, as well as what might be summarized as the phases of recognition, experimentation and accommodation in learning. We "perceive" art, "perceive" a question, "perceive" someone's motives. The sense is vague. In the case of art, as illustrated just above, the exposure amounts to more than a casual encounter; a change follows recognition of the import. The connotation of perceiving has to do with some sort of awareness as a response to stimuli, pointing to "mental" phenomena out of our reach. As art manifestly moves and transforms people, so may other things "perceived." But in art, the import remains concrete and autonomous; it has material and altogether objective reality. "Perception" of art discovers, not invents; it remains subject to verification, if not in regard to emotional impact, at least in its application to the fundamental structure of the work. It furthermore permits consensus. Experimentation, as the second phase of learning, in the case of art might be thought of as occurring during critical appraisal shared among several people. Critics seek at last to concur in their appreciations. The work of art is after all a tangible thing.

Exposure to environment, even if it does lead to "perception," would, in default of any further consequences, remain inaccessible to geographic understanding. Evidently, guessing at effects of such exposures will not do. Nor does an investigator's interpretation of a completed questionnaire, as he perceives it, based on responses to the gist of questions as perceived by respondents, offer reliable insights into the latter's perception of something. The logic loops around itself. The focus in this chapter, therefore, had to fall on "learning" rather than "perception."

The panorama of environmental learning shows it as ecologically adaptive and socially integrative. The process is transactional. Without assuming any special drives or motives, learning still appears a natural and necessary aspect of behavior, given certain pressures that implacably assert themselves on every human individual. The same pressures, or rather perhaps initiatives, may go so far as to account, in part at least, for some of the transactions that occur in the dissemination of cultural items and complexes.

Large variations appear in the extent of accommodation of behavior to environment. Human expression in some media, and notably in art, remains incomparably free. Thus man lives in two domains, and their dialectical interpenetration makes the very stuff of living. Geographers, in contemplating many lands and ways of life, can glimpse the riches of tradition founded in this dialectic. In doing so, they will encounter uniformities and recognize discrete divisions of mankind at home in their own territories. The origin and nature of such areal domains will occupy discussion next.

CHAPTER 6 *integration and expansion*

Communication designates an entity. The flow of information is an integrative process. In view of this, the invocation of the concept of "environment" can mislead. Separation drawn between a human individual and his surroundings, or between an object and its place, only serves the purpose of facilitating descriptions of the roles of several members interacting in ensembles. But the interaction presupposes wholeness. The linguistic act of decomposing integrated systems into parts cannot really disengage them from their situation. The most primitive of geographical categories distinguish simply "here" and "not here," and quantify the latter in terms of distance and direction; geography implicitly acknowledges the unity of place.

The foregoing paragraph should not be taken as a mere obeisance to holistic dogma. It states the fundamental premises that underlie the whole transactional-expressional interpretation of geography herein expounded. The key ideas bear summarizing. First, to say that an action takes place means to say that a situation changes. A deed, its effects, and its circumstances all snugly interlock. Second, the significance and identity of objects, and the character of persons, lie in what they do or might do; they define themselves in action and in use.

Upon this basis, further notions rest. The involvement of an individual in the social group, for instance, herein interpreted as consequent on sensory alertness and exposure, asks no conscious motivation. Likewise, physical activity within environment must *necessarily* occur in man as a living organism. Moreover, learning from such activity, as argued above, need represent no more than articulation of behavior with circumstance. Self-awareness and self-expression, finally, respond to needs for integration of the many very unlike, functionally complementary, individuals and groups within a society. The positions spelled out thus far do not assert that mankind has no mental life or will—they only avoid invoking any such assumptions. In fact, as plainly emerges from the discussion, the spirit—even if we shun the issue of its inner nature and its secret workings—manifests itself in guises so concrete and so objective as to leave its own indelible and shining mark on everything man touches. And caught in context, men respond to those objective manifestations and perpetuate their content in new works.

Experience, distilled into material expression of "ideas," can be communicated. The play between experience communicated and experience acquired by trial and error takes the form, in geographic terms, of relationships between site and situation factors, that is, between the actual life of man in a given place and the circulation of ideas current around it. The one supreme identity of all mankind is actual in the great unbroken chain of communication, unified in the spirit, capturing the world in its net. The other unities are local, fusing men into their habitats.

A community incorporates several different, simultaneous subsystems and linkages. It can grow, annex additional sectors, and enlist other members. The geographical growth involved may be technological, economic, or political in character, or a combination of these. Both the population and its ways and means of life spread in community growth. Not just ideas acquire a wider domain, but landscapes—tangible shapes. Sometimes, religious ideas and artistic styles concurrently spread, for example, under impetus from a community's vitality and power. The holistic conception of a community, essential to the present point, cannot overlook its technical basis. The complete, exhaustive integration of a population into the world about shows most clearly in the mechanical relationships between men and objects. In action, they make single unitary systems. The mechanistic model of a living community does not epitomize it, but does emphasize an important aspect of it. Technological systems, with men in fixed roles, can be analyzed descriptively to characterize a whole community. Livelihood activity, physiological human ecology, and technical operations are ways of conceiving dynamic relations with nature. The corresponding subsystems, attaining stability and durability, fasten themselves into environments and societies simultaneously. The resulting discrete patterns of modified environments, or of environmental modification, stand out as types.

Artificial environments, which are more or less under man's influence and whose features obey his requirements, take on varied patterns. We group them according to key strategies of livelihood, e.g., gathering, collecting, hunting and fishing, and agriculture in its various combinations with other activities. These strategies avail themselves of rather diverse technical means, so that many distinctive subtypes result, and of course in fitting into all sorts of special geographical circumstances, they differentiate still more. Some peculiarities of these artificial systems ought to be noted. Technique, unlike language or religion, can clearly vary in its relative convenience and productive efficiency. "Better" means something definite in conjunction with this one phase of culture. Technical systems fall into indisputable ranking on the basis of energy available per person, food production per capita or per hectare, and similar criteria. Front-runners in productivity may even regard themselves as above the rest of humanity. Furthermore, technical capacities—both "know-how" and capital equipment—increase cumulatively. This inheritance keeps growing—"the rich gets richer." Finally, technical systems tend to expand spatially, as remarked. It would appear, now, that these technical properties jointly and steadily cause an acceleration of progress in certain areas initially favored, and produce a declining gradient of efficiency and prosperity around them. Only catastrophic changes can redress such gradients running from rich to poor.

The arrayal of past technologies still registers on the culture-map. Thus the distribution of agriculture has epicenters in the putative earliest centers of seed farming, Mesopotamia and Mexico, along with "root-crop" hearths in Southeast Asia and the Andes. Cities, again, center in the lower Tigris-Euphrates Valley. Less efficient or not so progressive techniques and settlement patterns cling to the margins, and the gradients swoop out and down to them. North Atlantic countries form another epicentric zone for later progress, likewise garlanded with underdeveloped countries, whose wealth they extracted for their own expansion.

The overall expansiveness of technical progress goes along with that of given systems, closely unified by communication. For at whatever level of technological finesse livelihood embraces and embroils a group of persons, the more advanced the system, by and large, the more numerous the group. Moreover, such a system consists or resides in specific material features, of determinate types and necessary attributes. A livelihood system must control and draw upon stated natural resource supplies to live. It also needs secure communication routes, lands for agriculture, gathering, or the chase, manufacturing facilities, and centers for storage, maintenance, and distribution of products and for service. Each system imposes precise and necessary geographical requirements. Deprived of its geographical basis of sites and routes, it collapses. The pitiless ruination of aboriginal hunting grounds and working places in North America or Australia, attendant on the white man's impetuous grasping for land, springs immediately to mind. Hardly less inexorable has been the continuing eviction of the poorer people of North American cities in the course of "redevelopment," removing the needed base of one group's life to make way for another's different scale.

This geography of outrage merits more attention than it gets. A historical geography of European expansion, if the indigenous victims receive their fair notice, is grisly. Undoubtedly the spread of other geographically expansive peoples, e.g., the Han Chinese or the Aztecs, not to mention the Mongols and the cannibal Zande, has equally dark chapters. Such ugly episodes reflect, in large degree, the resource and communication needs of the aggressors' technologies, for the sake of which another livelihood pattern may have suffered disastrous disruption, and its dependents extermination or at best assimilation.

In technical expansions, social relations and communication operate through wider and wider territories, to bring new uses of the land and new facilities. A productive system, when it takes over, makes over. Consequently, very definite and tangible geographic change ensues. The alterations of the land trace out the progress of cultural dispersal and later diversification and in fact provide some of the best evidence for them. Moreover, introduction of new technical regimes implies establishment of a new symbolism in landscape. (To the native the "improvements" that grow up are sadly eloquent.)

At times, the technological incentives for expansion and the incorporation of new territory center on resources, at other times on communications, and yet again sometimes on market areas and privileges. All such objectives overlap. The ancient Egyptians and Assyrians left behind copious records of expeditions to obtain rare natural raw materials. At other times, the same conquerors seized ports, or laid hold of strategic passes and oases on the trade routes. Occasionally, complementarity might be sought: access for northerly countries to tropical crops, for example, or control of the minerals of a mountainous country by plainsmen. Later, quantity became crucial. The development of industry in large units brought a vast-scale increase in the demand for resources, with results needless to detail.

Economic complementarity has provided a rationale not only for full incorporation of new areas into productive systems, but even more, for trade. Each area, under such a system, relies on many others. So goes the theory, often violated in practice. Along with area complementarity, emphasis on the most profitable line of production supposedly enables an economy to gain the greatest return. Comparative advantage encourages allocation of areas to specialty production, and thus favors geographic diversity. To the degree that organized and influential economic relations really affect a major area, they contribute very much toward breaking it up into specialized productive units. But of course this only obtains when communication and exchange flourish. Then, indeed, a rather predictable progress of geographic differentiation occurs.

Exchanges and Migrations

Exchange, the economic or material phase of the general communication phenomenon, conforms to some special principles. It is sensitive, more than some other sorts of communication, to terrain and distance, for it involves the laborious physical movement of goods. Even so, the hazard and toil of transport may be borne if the exchange yields enough gain. Herein lies the crux: exchange goes two ways, to the advantage of both parties. As communication, it has the peculiar feature of occurring only when parity obtains between the two sides' contributions. Whereas this condition surely prevents a flow as free as that of words or ideas, entrepreneurs leap in with great gusto and overcome all manner of hideous obstacles, when profit promises. The reciprocating exchange pattern therefore operates in a very selective way, to bind together only certain persons and areas that balance each other in some way. It has no full parallel among other sorts of communications. Further, trade is particularly sensitive to social instability and disorganization. Traders want regular links and outlets. Hence, a skeleton of well-used, enduring, and relatively secure avenues of movement, over which dissemination of all kinds of goods and cultural ideas moves, has become established over time.

For example, the prehistoric trade in amber, salt, copper, and tin laid foundations for many later routes of communication in Europe and the Near East. From the Baltic shores, some amber moved westward across the North European Plain, but the chief "amber road" ran southward overland along the Central European rivers and then over the Carpathians or Alpine passes to debouch at the head of the Adriatic. Eastward it would have followed an ancient routeway down the Danube. Amber, along with honey, furs, and Ural gold, also must have come down the Volga system. Eastern Anatolian copper moved by land south- and westward to Bronze Age smiths. From the island of Cyprus, named for the metal, it reached them by sea. Traffic also by sea linked the almost mythical tin lands of northwest Spain, Cornwall, and Brittany with the ancient and even preliterate Mediterranean. Ancient seaways coasted East Africa likewise, bearing a succession of traders: Egyptians to the land of Punt; Semites to the incense-isles; later, Omanis and Persians to Sofala. Once adequate craft had developed, other seafarers made for Malabar and maintained a sailing traffic that still lives. On Oriental seas, the same spice traffic led east from Malabar and Coromandel to Malacca. There it met another passageway that skirted eastern Asia. By land, the great Silk Road crossed Inner Asia by way of Tarim, and branched to reach the Black Sea east of Trebizond, and the Mediterranean in Syria. A major route for gold and ivory ran down the Nile and another passed across the sands by way of Timbuktu. Across Europe lay a fur route, from east to west along the moraines and the south margin of the North European Plain, linking on the east with the Volga, and meeting the Channel and the radiating riverways of France.

The corresponding network in America has left less clear remains, especially because the decline in native population broke the continuity of development. Oceangoing native craft definitely had found sea routes along the northwestern coasts of North America, throughout the Caribbean, and up and down the tropical west coasts at least from Guatemala to Peru. Overland trails connected the basins of the Columbia and Colorado rivers with the Great Plains, and major water routes threaded through the Great Lakes and down the large river valleys. Lines of communication of course attained appropriately more elaboration in civilized Middle America and the Andes.

Such communication lines and regular trade routes could just as well become avenues of expansion. The trader himself might double as a brigand, or alternatively as a permanent settler. Merchants always played an ambiguous role. The ships that plied the Levantine or Eastern seas in search of pirate plunder might meekly barter for cargoes when outfought or outbluffed. A vessel and a party strong enough to protect a valuable cargo might well excel as a raiding force. Caravaneers could support themselves by either taking tribute or transporting goods for hire, indifferently. The origins of the specialized nomadic groups and partially itinerant guilds can only go back to their breaking away from more stable, sedentary communities as marginal operators, adventurers, or outlaws. In good times, those who drove the flocks might wander back; in harder days they might abandon settled life and graze their beasts on distant pastures, or engage themselves in the carriage of commodities, or indulge in raids and pillaging. The life of Old World desert tribes appears to accommodate all these options simultaneously. The maritime traditions known from the shores of Eurasia likewise embrace a spectrum of activities and inclinations, from fishing to trading to piracy, most of them anchored in some coastal agricultural community. The maritime history of the Japanese and Norse exemplifies the pattern. In these situations, the trade, to count for much, must deal in precious goods—exactly as the plundering did. Indeed, for all but some exceptional periods of history (e.g., the *pax romana* by land and by sea; the ordered calm of Achaemenian Persia, or the nineteenth century when British naval power at its acme guarded trade), the line between the predatory and pacific aspects of these mobile occupations always tended to fade or waver with momentary circumstances.

Commercial intercourse, however, meant a lasting bond. The importance of trading routes and traders' outposts to the march of culture is incalculable. Sea lanes served as major avenues not only for exchange of goods, of course, but for dissemination of ideas. Many a people with only a puny foothold on the land was able, by its maritime expansion, to take root in a widespread domain, consisting of port colonies and coastal stretches, whence its culture could infiltrate the adjacent inland areas. In this manner the Phoenicians established themselves on Spanish, Sicilian, and North African shores, founding enduring societies in Tartessus, Utica, and Carthage. Greek seafarers in a similar way colonized the coasts of southern Italy, Sicily, Cyprus, and the Black Sea litoral. Sea traders from India, and from the Hadramaut, Oman, and Persia left substantial colonies and influence in Southeast Asia and East Africa, respectively. Spreading inland behind shore cities, the culture of the colonies dispersed to some extent among the inhabitants, but not enough in any case to transform thoroughly a really large area for long. The impact of the native hinterland peoples on the traders of the sea proved even less significant, for maritime colonies retain the old home ways, since their most substantial communication remains oriented to other ports and especially to those of their close kinfolk. Even to this day, maritime character in a city is equated with variety and with a "cosmopolitan" atmosphere. Despite the lack of full cultural amalgamation, nonetheless, the "sea-webs" of the traders have profoundly conditioned cultural history.

As much might be said of nomads and caravan drivers. Unlike the seafarers, however, the wanderers of steppe and desert may blend with their cultivating neighbors. Or they may themselves sow an occasional crop in some isolated ravine, to be harvested later on the returning swing of their pastoral cycle; the caravan men may even base themselves in a city and tend gardens. But these are no farmers, no real house dwellers. Unlike maritime colonists as a rule, the nomads proper absorb far more from the peoples they meet and trade with or rob than they give to them. Nomad tribes' artifacts are imitations. They equip themselves scantily and derivatively. Their art, in some cases carrying certain motifs and techniques to a peerless development, like that of ancient Luristan and the Scythian animal style, perpetuated rather "primitive" traits along with multiple outside influences. But the peoples of desert and steppe, such as the Turks, the Arabs, and the Tuareg and Moors, acted as cultural postmen for their agricultural neighbors on all sides. Even the most uncouth of desert tribesmen, as they migrated about, could carry new ideas between the more civilized fringes of their realms, and these explicitly intermediary groups deserve credit for enormous transferrals of ideas as well as goods from China westward, from the Mediterranean into Black Africa, and from the Middle East outward in all directions. The lack of such long-distance migrators and traders in the New World seems to be responsible for cultural segmentation between the North American Pacific Coast, particularly native California, and the rest of the Continent, and possibly also for abiding primitivity in southern South America and the farther rimlands of Australia.

Thus do livelihood patterns that involve mobility portend cultural dissemination. The continuing apartness of the peoples concerned, culturally and otherwise, does not vitiate their influence on neighbors. Now, another and far more extensive regime of livelihood, agriculture, plays an even larger role in the spread of culture. Agricultural communities, as their population grows, take more land under cultivation. Their holdings extend. New settlements grow up when the distance from the old village to the field becomes prohibitive. These new settlements become foci for infestation of additional areas. By slow increments the cultivators' domain expands, passing imperturbably around major barriers, leaping over small obstacles, pushing out in all directions to the absolute limits determined by climate or terrain. As they go, they clear, and ultimately they may also devastate. The forest recedes, the swamps are drained and diked, the dry lands watered. Agricultural expansion progresses for centuries, sometimes only to suffer arrest and recession through famine, warfare, epidemic, or flood; then the forests, dunes, and marshes reappear, to await renewed conquest by the farmers. Pulsations of advance and retreat have occurred in many areas repeatedly. France, Germany, and Greece have been cleared several times. Each time some irreversible changes have been wrought, however, and some relics of each settlement remain.

The cultivators' elemental tide encounters impediments from human enemies as well as from nature. Thus the southern Russian steppe has seen a succession of farming occupations, armatured by thriving river traffic on the Volga, Don, and Dnepr, rise in alternation with a nomad dominance that swept away the farmers and even their cities. The pertinent archaeological evidence would suggest that this pulsation has continued down from prehistoric times. Analogous tension between the *Sahel* borderlands of agriculture and the wanderers' Sahara, on the inner fringes of Maghreb in northwestern Africa, affords confirmation of this dynamism. Again, there could be no grander, sadder tragedy than that of thickly populated farming tracts in Central America that have dwindled to nothing, giving way to unbroken brushland or rain forest, since the Spaniards arrived. The natives perished in battle, or died of epidemics, or had their foodstocks entirely and fatally requisitioned, or were conscripted to work in distant mines or plantations. Similar catastrophe befell the Greater Antilles, but there at least the conquerors did trouble to possess and repopulate the land. Hence, as farming settlement can expand so solidly, it can also vanish. As culture spreads in this way, it also may wane and leave behind its mute and lonely monuments amid the forest, like the Mexican temples of the Gulf Coast and the great stone idols and fine little gold figures of the Caribbean plains of Central America.

Some of the farmers' remains are doubtless more enduring than those of the nomad conquerors, more like the splendor of cities bequeathed by the seafarers. They differ through breach of tradition, when whole rural societies are wiped out or vanish, from the cities, whose vigorous life persists, absorbing in folklore and habit the legacy left by millennia of intercourse. Yet the more lasting architectural and engineering works even of extinct farming cultures often dominate, and are the pride of, modern countries. What would Peru or Turkey or Cambodia be without their ruins?

The everlasting sediments of history, dropped by fleeting currents of migration, trade, and settlement, like materials jettisoned by moving water gradually compacting into recognizable deposits, form an analogous kind of stratified column accessible to study and interpretation.

The meaning of such cultural sequences for scholarship, however, is dwarfed by their continuing impact on societies and cultures of living people, wherever occupation of the land continues or has reoccurred. For landscapes accumulate and deepen; the past mounts up. In ancient places, life becomes increasingly embedded in a predetermined matrix of expression. The intrusion into daily life of references from former occupation, often surely quite recast and reinterpreted, must be considerable; or do gigantic temples and statues seem to modern, uninstructed peasants simply parts of a supine, banal nature? We have no warrant for believing that the living common people need revere, or even remember, the makers of their landscape. Nonetheless, such dominating features as the ancient temples, terraces, or mounds must mean something to them, albeit something mythical and other than their true allusion. Their symbolism may be freshly manufactured, and what passes for their history in fact may be a baseless legend. Yet any such presences necessarily make up part of an environment's expression. Many a landscape's brooding figures and obsolete constructions must have lent plausibility to fantasy, and incubated legends of a misty past.

The landscape expressions attending the spread of cultivators or seaborne merchant peoples have other sides to them beside the workaday aspect. Their monuments are intimations of a higher culture too. And the expressive force behind such monuments stems from the social vitality of whole peoples, organized and extensive. They attest a political order. Whether integrated by a religious elite of scribes and priests, a warrior caste, or a merchant oligarchy, some kind of state organization develops in any such relatively advanced society, given the necessary density of settlement and communication and the appropriate technology.

The Geographical Careers of States

The administrative apparatus of the state patronizes expansion and integration, and presides over the internal functioning of a society. It allocates precedence and jurisdiction to persons, institutions, functions; mobilizes forces for common tasks; adjudicates disputes and conflicts; and enshrines the collective identity. These roles seem commonplace; the more arresting one, less noticed, consists in giving an ensured context and orientation to the lives of its subjects. Such states, with acquiescence, grow up from nations, i.e., peoples who willingly share their ultimate values. A state is a unique and exclusive structure endowed with its own territory. Long divided thus, the Western world has latterly extended the state-system as one of its most characteristic and tenacious impositions upon non-Western areas. The state, however, in many areas arose independently. Political consolidation had proceeded far in Africa and native America long before conquest by Europeans, to say nothing of the complicated structures of southern and eastern Asia. All in all, the associated territorial system represents one of the most fundamental facts of all geography, both cultural and otherwise. Integrated areas predominate.

The soul of a state is communication. As the pre-eminent form of institution among a people, the political apparatus dominates and infiltrates all others. It creates and wields its own instruments of force within subordinate military and police institutions. It often pre-empts, and coalesces with, the main religious institution, utilizing it as agent, and its creed as apologia, for power. It insinuates itself into the economic system and turns the latter to its own ends. All of these conquests, annexations, and subordinations result from the capture of primacy in communication, along with the power that defends and enforces rule. The media of intercourse are dear and vital to the state. Mechanisms of cultural dissemination, expansion, and integration, discussed herein, deeply involve state systems, and even many of the symbols in environments stand for the might and the myths of states. All this amounts, in one sense, to acknowledging that peoples—not just families, not just residents of each immediate locality, and not just livelihood or interest groups, but whole diverse and widespread populations—cast their common lot around a larger group identity and purpose. A multinational state, a national one, or even an essentially tribal state, may embody such purpose and identity. Communications and power will always preoccupy it.

The deeper reality of political and territorial unity surely has to do with more than the assumption of power by the few. A relatively strong bond of comprehension and solidarity among persons is a prerequisite of a meaningful life. The state or nation (or its simpler primitive equivalent) embodies and expounds the socially supreme "rules of the game," the code of values underlying action and judgment, and the penalties and rewards going along with their application to life. The prizes and forfeits for individual performance and display, in the contest and drama of living, derive from the ultimate meanings vouched for by the collectivity and vested in national symbols and institutions. As inferred in an earlier chapter, virtue needs an audience; the sense of reality needs a domicile. A nation—as "mutual admiration society"—compels credence and allegiance. Thus a state, standing for values sacred to a nation, may demand sacrifice and undivided loyalty. If man cannot attach himself wholeheartedly to some evaluating group, he can attach himself nowhere, to nothing. If he cannot live within a common world among appreciative others, he might as well not regard his life at all. Even those whose supposed commitment is to mankind as a whole must recite their oath of allegiance to supreme mankind in some one language, and justify it in some single set of value terms.

The nation, equivalent to a society united on the elective basis of common values and a common medium for their expression, and the state—the same in power—assure communication, through fostering the acceptance of their symbolic media and vehicles. Sovereign states tend to impose their language upon their own subjects, alien in speech or otherwise. Everyone must show compliance with ceremonial, deference to symbols, obedience to officials, involvement in associations and activities. Allegiance and conformity indeed, at times, become major vehicles of personal display and worth. But the reassuring rituals of solidarity have an ugly side. Someone is always trying to force the stranger to kiss the flag or march with the crowd. The real point is then lost, for these symbols of solidarity normally have a strongly positive, unifying value. They enable men to cooperate, and individually to strive for achievement. Without common symbols, how could men understand one another? How could they esteem and encourage one another?

The much more prosaic, mundane aspects of the state's or nation's role probably have equal importance. A unified, communicating people, technological entity, or economy, demands physical means and regular procedures. The political institution, coordinating and enforcing, provides for establishment and maintenance of roads, ports, canals, markets. State initiative prompts the building of ships, the outfitting of caravans, the creation of a regular post and courier service. Throughout recorded history, great systems of communication have been instituted and managed by central power. The Spaniards marveled at the roads, post stations, public storehouses, and rapid coast-to-mountain courier services of Peru, as Herodotus had earlier praised Persia's. Medieval friars gaped in awe at the Mongol messenger and police system, as later visitors praised imperial communication in China. Government intervention in nineteenth-century England or the United States, in undertakings such as canal development and railroad building, emphatically was nothing new. But state involvement with all sorts of technical communication has expanded, e.g., in telephone systems, highways, air service, communication satellites.

In addition to the impetus and support they give to expanding communications, governments have been at pains to provide security of movement over them. Many a sea power evolved in the course of suppressing piracy. A struggle against highwaymen has usually marked the history of emerging land powers, parallel with equally violent campaigns against marauders, mostly retreating and embattled native peoples, along frontiers. China faced these problems under many dynasties, as did ancient Assyria or Aztec Mexico, as much as the United States. The guarantee of order, premise of successful communication, becomes a chief rationale for exercise of public force.

Not only order, but "law and order." Any state of consequence has an instituted legal system, governing not only public peace and safety but property. Laws reconcile conflicting interests, but above all project agreed stability into prospective events, and thus encourage venturing. Law defines the future. The protection of property and the promotion of exchange, in many different societies at various times and places, have inspired like laws. The great codes often resemble each other in spirit. Over and above the law itself, fixed procedures in general developed under state patronage. Upon the legal basis grew up such devices to facilitate communication and exchange as coinage, weights and measures, and accounting, all of them also subserving unity.

Schooling became another care, first of unifying institutions of religion, then of states. The indoctrination of young people with a group's tradition, needless to say, does not wait upon a public institution, but as communication has intensified, notably in the modern world, and nations and peoples have been drawn into closer union, the concern for standardization has increased. Public schooling helped the state to rise to pervasive and definitive control over all other social forms and levels. Schools have often aided in eliminating or enfeebling voices of defiance and dissent, which had remained entrenched wherever language, religion, or tradition diverged. Unanimity of values and purposes thus came closer to realization. Enforced state formation has recently, however, drastically outrun the spontaneous formation of voluntary national units. The schools go in as pioneers of nationhood. The early generation of graduates, pawns to the national dream, act as exponents and executors of the state ideal. Such has been the case of old (e.g., the mandarins and the oddly-recruited janissaries) and it still holds.

A geography of states today exhibits vast disparities. Many states coincide with self-aware and long-constituted nations, i.e., peoples who share clear-cut territory, values, and activity. At another extreme, some states represent impositions of fictitious unity at an extensive scale over a fine mosaic of much smaller, dissident and dissonant, tribal units. Whereas a polyglot African state exists at the scale of a complex and areally vast combination of unlike, but parallel, ecological domains and livelihood patterns, threaded through with at most a European-conferred transport and communication net, sometimes its component tribal units alone can enlist the loyalty of their own people, focusing on one manner of existing in one kind of environment. In such new states, an urban commercial and proletarian element and a foreign-oriented elite, as well as the army and the bureaucracy, stand for the national as against the tribal interests and values. Only if a preponderant majority of subjects can crystallize around the former, nontribal elements and share their sentiments do the states have good prospects. In these cases, the close connection among economy, ecology, and communications asserts itself powerfully.

African states do not stand alone in this regard. Much of Asia exemplifies a similar disproportion between local and national organization. In Asia, however, the situation features, within the boundaries of individual sovereignties, a combination of strong, advanced, cohesive, dominant nationalities, with fragmented, backward, weaker minorities. Certain rice-rich southeast Asian flood and coastal plains support the dominant Burmans, Thais, Cambodians, and Vietnamese in the respective mainland countries, and on Taiwan the Chinese, in the Philippines the Tagalogs, Visayans, and Ilocanos, and in Indonesia the Javanese and

Sundanese, in heavy dominance as against the sparser, poorer, very much divided hill tribes and out-islanders. Even the eastern and northern marches of India and Pakistan and some of the hill country of the northern Deccan harbor similar mosaics of minorities. The scale of organization here again exhibits great political disparity between the hills and the productive lowlands, to say nothing of enormous cultural contrasts. Even in the American countries, certain corelands have historically predominated over other areas, so that almost every nation focuses upon a particular small region, and the neglected and largely empty (or at least relatively unincorporated) peripheries count for little.

The concept of the nation corresponds to a certain aspect of a people, under which its choice of emphasis and membership is free. A nation exists without force. If the true nations of the world were mapped, how many would we count? Some, like the Jews, have lived millennia in exile; others dwell submerged and only gradually awake to a new identity, exploding into reality as pride comes alive in them. Nations form and reform, merge and diverge. Yesterday's Indian tribes may tomorrow arise as a single new nation in North America. When a people discovers itself and lays claim to a home and a destiny, declaring its independence and fighting its revolutionary war, a state begins and a new order prevails. How many such peoples have dearly bought independence, only to forfeit freedom!

Expansion and integration of peoples contribute to, but do not dominate, the spread of culture. No matter what the centralizing appeal or force, the local community by its own momentum tends to drift away in spirit and in practice from the standard ways. The massive presence of older elements in landscapes and of other influences in society beside the national ones induces variation. Experience *in situ* teaches different lessons than accepted texts. And so, as in the case of dialects that rise spontaneously within a language's domain, or superstitions and mumbo jumbo seeping into orthodox religion, culture takes on a different color, a different tone, in every setting. A nation has a multitude of faces; a people after all is many people.

Some reason exists, in fact, for wondering how much the nation really means in daily life. In a country like the United States, at least until the 1950's, nationhood and participation in it went for granted, and few of a normal person's acts had any conscious relation to the nation as such. In more embattled situations and especially in smaller, neighbor-conscious nations of the Old World the case was otherwise. But only the few could involve themselves deeply in nationhood as, in itself, a way of life. The communication functions that tied it together and maintained it became merely technical operations, and the symbols graven into the landscapes and entwined in all behavior lost their vividness. Both the concept and the connections that make the nation a reality recede, and only the sterner, starker mechanisms of the state its enforcer stay openly and urgently in view. When the people have become thus oblivious to the common values and directions of group life, and turned their gaze from the collective to the individual and local identity, it appears that cataclysmic dramas come to the fore to reaffirm the nation's claims upon its people. Wars and repressions reassert the collective identity. They contribute to revival and perpetuation of particular states, as well as to the birth of new ones. A crusade against the infidels, a purge of alleged traitors, a witch hunt, a pogrom—such recurrent barbarities, too, may bear some relationship to the importunate need of a given established hierarchy or leadership to take a tight new grasp on a people slipping from it.

A war represents a geographical game of communication, each adversary pushing and probing to break through and annex territories to his own communication network, subjecting them thereby to his own cultural and political sovereignty. The metallic violence of the armies only operates until, after annexation, the velvet violence of peacetime police and the law become established. The war itself, or the persecution, enlists the sacrifice and also emphatically the pride of a people. Lethal glory is sought after; pain and hatred are both exalted. In the case of war, the whole citizenry, or the chosen ones considered worthy of battle, rush to immolate themselves. Those remaining at home work and weep for the heroes. Symbols of the nation emerge and are paraded, those of the enemy derided and defiled. Selves cast themselves into entirely new and far more grandiose roles; the battlefield stalwarts share in the general emulation along with management wizards, overtime workers, and the fungal proliferation of profiteers and prostitutes. In the case of a persecution, on the other hand, the bigoted and the treacherous achieve their glory. There are no heroes, only informers and hangmen; no glory, only unclean frenzy. But campaigns against Catholics, Jews, Albigensians, Moslems, Hindus, Buddhists, and many such groups have stained the pages of history. The preponderance of religious communities among persecutors is notable, although not unrelieved. The rationale, apparently, requires heavenly sanctions, no earthly motive for such undertakings being credible. But both national wars and religious persecutions have served the sense of nationhood well. Europe spent most of its historical career in religious wars, and this peculiar feature of its past, perhaps, uniquely equipped it to forge its unusual institutional form, the purely national state.

Geopolitical Questions

Reflection on the state, given the ways that culture spreads, inescapably suggests geopolitical questions. Do regular processes of dissemination and standardization favor certain specific areal forms for nations or states? Are particular areas and nations inherently congruent?

Conceiving the origin and life of nations dialectically, they appear to express a play between the tendency of the state to unite the communications of an ever-expanding area in a single system on the one hand, and a tendency of geographic circumstances to impose strict spatial limits where costs of integration prove excessive on the other. A state grows as big as it can. The capacity to organize and manage areal networks, and the ability to implant an effective national symbolism, both play their role. Therefore size tends to reach a maximum limit as steeper and steeper gradients of cost or difficulty, measured commonly against increasing distance from the core, are encountered; furthermore, the state will eventually meet absolute obstacles to its advance.

In actuality, most nations tend to attain their limits with the boundaries of major linguistic units or religious domains. Only rarely does true, voluntary unity surpass these areal dimensions. Unification of a linguistic or religious character does not, however, automatically proceed nor, having been achieved, does it always lead to harmony and unanimity. But ethnic nationalism having been in vogue for several centuries now, true national territories have become the rule in many regions. Given the propensity of language areas to disaggregate, centralizing processes must remain sedulously at work to hold even such an area together as a nation. The relative lack of barriers to internal communication may give way to alienation as separate dialects contest the central language, or as incompatible religious tendencies develop.

The dissemination of cultural content, and hence the formation of distinct cultural areas, relies mostly on institutions. Logically, therefore, even ethnic distribution will tend ultimately to reflect the areal patterns of present or former institutions. Specifically, in modern times, the most relevant institutional complexes, subsuming most of the others, are states. The consolidating role of the state, already noted, defines a potential area; work and power realize it. Through force, the state compels adherence of new areas; through developing communications, it binds them in. In addition to the political and military problem of the feasible extension of a state, the technical and economic one imposes itself. Communications, that is, their concrete aspect as road and railroad links, canals and harbors, signal systems, goods transport, and so on, reduce to engineering projects. Terrain, especially, is their censor and referee. Accordingly, the physical features of the earth, apart from their effect on the state's use of military and police force (also exerted mostly through communication), may reasonably be expected at certain junctures to interpose barriers to regular communication so forbidding as to bound the tenable domain. Hence the potential limits must tend to register alike an ethnic factor, military capabilities, and engineering feasibilities. Conversely, particular physical circumstances are often alleged to justify or at least to favor expansion of a state's communications and the incorporation of a given area.

American "manifest destiny," the alleged "urge to the sea" of the

Muscovites, the old Polish dream of a kingdom spanning from Black Sea to Baltic, and many other examples of politically momentous determinist doctrines may come to mind. Their sometimes pernicious appeal and result ought not to obscure the possible truths underlying them, however. Unpalatable as it may seem, a compact and homogeneous geographical area, well served by routes of intercourse, favors cultural unity and often shows it. In contrast, a rugged, uneven area very often exhibits high ethnic diversity. An ecologically stable fragmentation into many self-sustaining small population clusters, such as is common in tropical countries, where interareal communication remains difficult and incentives for trading are slight, can aggravate separatism. Political consolidation has to attend to its geographical foundations.

Even shape counts, if rather ambiguously. It comes as no great surprise that groups of islands—e.g., the British Isles, the Philippines—have frequently constituted political units, but conversely many island chains harbor ethnic variety. Nations and states like France, Russia, or Brazil have developed around radial waterway frameworks; in the latter example, however, the rule fails to apply fully, since the population hugs only the coast. Land-based states ought supposedly to stop at water barriers, but in actuality many of them have straddled important straits; witness England with its long command of the Cinque Ports, Denmark holding Scania across the Strait, or Spain and its former slice of Morocco. Ethnic groups often hold similar positions, like the Bering Strait Eskimo, the Malays of Malacca, and formerly the Yemenis at the Bab el Mandeb on the Red Sea. River valleys, too, ambiguously either unify or divide: the Habsburg monarchy ruled Danubia—now its central artery has become recurrently a boundary feature. The foregoing cases document the unreliability of easy generalizations in this matter. Yet terrain and its shape undoubtedly do play a part in national and cultural evolution.

The expansion of a nation or a state does not take place in a void. Since Upper Paleolithic times, when mankind succeeded in distributing itself into all the continents, frontiers have more and more constricted, and groups have come into ever more intimate proximity. Expansion of one folk implies the withdrawal or subjugation of another. Even what the enthusiasts call "God's country" turns out to have belonged to some hapless fellow men before. Consequently, a major element in the processes herein considered is the counterpressure from neighbors. Only small and sparsely populated domains can afford a cordon of empty neutral territory around them; buffer zones are expensive, and tempting to aggressors. Despite the declared inadequacy of generalizations about particular states and nations as subsisting geographic entities, certain major geographical units do seem to persist as culturally distinct. The oceans have always sufficiently impeded intercourse, despite their usefulness for trade, that they continue as first-order limits. The large deserts and high mountain ranges, even when themselves inhabited, constitute second-order barriers. Sub-Saharan Africa, Transalpine Europe, and peninsular India are enduring realities. Yet lesser barriers cannot stay the flux of power, and cultural and political systems swell and shrink territorially in tight contiguity to other growing and declining systems. Boundaries ceaselessly shift, as if forever seeking to anchor themselves geographically. Units form and dissolve. Peoples crystallize and dissolve again within others, all constantly changing. Culture pulsates and presses against the boundaries of each cellular domain within the geographic tissue of humanity.

Human history, as we conceive it normally, centers on the territorial drama of integration and expansion, chronicling successive systems, disclosing their conflicts, accounting for their destinies. Even in the blind, titanic history of states contending, the explanations and interpretations inveterately depend on individual ambition and initiative. History is made by men, or rather by selves. The same selfhood that strains to assert itself in a work of art, a well-tended garden, or a modern skyscraper, moves all of history. Whether it supposedly find its motive agency in love of fame and sense of public honor, in the prompting of the gods, in libido, or in class consciousness, the expressive impulse dominates and organizes.

The spread of culture, like that of power, operates through personal expression. As political rule and military conquest ordain and enforce a master's way, so does cultural influence or assimilation instruct the pupil in the teacher's way. Probably if left to impersonal chance, culture would hardly spread or develop; once established, a way of life would fossilize. Only by personal exertions can constant cultural dissemination be fully accounted for. But those exertions, if they are to bear fruit, probably rather impose than merely offer new habits. Without insistence on a standard that is centrally enforced, continuity would suffer constant and fatal disruption; no permanent, predictable result would ensue from communication. Substantial culture change, as against mere passing fashion, is likely to emerge from situations of some sort of inequality between the partners involved. Power, wealth, or prestige evidently weigh in the adoption of new ideas. The really notable examples of cultural assimilation or strong cultural influence show a fairly consistent association with political or social domination. "Imperialism" in its ordinary sense appears to produce cultural change in directions reflecting the preference and convenience of the dominant "imperial" elites. Roman, Persian, Chinese, Spanish, Russian, British—"empires" mean a great deal culturally. The designation "cultural imperialism" may fairly apply to the one single process having most effect in altering major cultural distributions. The explicitly constituted "empires" in themselves account for a mighty lot of striking patterns. Similar super-institutions, by other names, remain at work. The policy of the imperial power, entailing recruitment of additional subjects, appropriation of further resources, and securing of new military advantages, calls for incorporation of people into its system; communication and development demand cultural integration keeping pace with territorial expansion. Hence the patterns of individual lives become subject not only to the vagaries of nature and the native cultural regime, but to these larger movements and transformations.

Such speculations as this theme has introduced challenge the alert imagination, but they are not primarily the issue for this study. The roles of individual experience, choice, and action within cultural geographic context remain to be summarized.

CHAPTER 7
location and communication

Communication makes all mankind one and every man unique. The person evolves through involvement. A ceaseless circulation of ideas, seeping through environmental filters, reaches everyone, and almost everyone, at least for fading moments, manages to cast back something with his signature upon it. The net effect of endless individual acts of interpretation and initiative is perpetually to re-sort, recast, and redirect the fluid substance of culture.

Every human being stands for an unrepeatable personal past, and acts in inimitable circumstances. You may call the residue of each man's personal geography and history the freedom of the will, or equally consider it the working of a fine, exact necessity. But no man's actions have true duplicates. Immersed in a turbulent nature, implicated with other men, an individual must move and act, learn and relate. He responds to the pressures—but chooses his way. The infinitesimal determinacies, if such they be, that fix men's acts and lives in practice make them absolute, inscrutable, unique. Human choices thus elude our finest calculation. We can only let our sentient selves, as instruments, attune themselves to what our fellow men express, and hope that reason reads true order into it.

Enviromental content and connections shape experience, and hence behavior. Such is the whole gist of the argument thus far. Empathy and rational insight probably clarify the import of environment enough that most human behavior becomes intelligible, if not quite expectable, once its circumstances are grasped. A cultural geography at its best illuminates behavior in this manner. The virtue of it does not simply lie in making other people understandable; it can also cast light on one's own acts in their context.

The individual and his environment, equally physical (or "geographical") and social, although treated as two separate realities for discussion, in fact are one. A person and his context and actions, as well as a people and its environment, had best be seen as indivisible. The members of a society interlock in their behavior, each one bounding and defining others, each act meaningful as it relates to other acts. Because of the tight unity obtaining, any isolating measurement becomes, by disrupting it, an artificial one. Yet we cannot conveniently conceive this unity in the terms of ordinary thought. The analytic bias in us all inclines to blind us to the entirety of things.

Geography divides the world into regions, and deals with individual places, whereas in fact the world is one continuum, and any place is just a focus, blending into its vicinity. A man's behavior, too, belongs within a total phenomenon of human behavior. Furthermore, the information that passes from one person to another in communication does not itself represent a discrete entity, but may again be seen as part of a continuous flux. Culture designates more a process or a property of a dynamical system than a static set of separate ideas. As it moves, culture takes on new states and aspects, as does the medium of community in which it circulates.

The holistic viewpoint envisions each individual acting in perpetual coordination with his fellows, and all of them in like manner interacting with their surroundings. The adjustments among members in this highly articulated unity become the stuff of communication.

Individual human selfhood lies always at another crossing point of a career with a context of action. The individual, under that one of his aspects that is the person, consists of a social phenomenon: a human being located, occupied, distinguishable within the social manifold. ("Person" is accordingly a perceptual term.) The located, integrated human "person" conceived within society corresponds to the human "organism" conceived as a material being within nature. Society and nature make a double, or rather, a redundant single context. Under its subjective other aspect, the "self" is a continuity, not located, but measured in time. Just as its environment is compounded of other beings spatially arrayed, the being of the self compounds environments through time.

The world remakes itself through the intermediary of man. For each human individual, in his own geographical and historical position, receives from all the world around him the manifold communication that suffuses it, perceiving significance both in other men's unequivocal expressions and in faint fancies of his own read into nature. Responding, testing, he acquires concrete experience in context; learning and developing, he acts. As he acts, experience becomes idea, a shape for things, to be expressed in turn through his own unfolding communication. He manipulates his environment to reveal and proclaim his experience. Thus is the world, impressing itself upon a man, reshaped in its turn by his expression. But he, too, is transformed.

The sources of vivid experience appeal; the opportunities for discovery attract. Human curiosity decides lives. Men's choices show likewise the force of longing for community. Life grows toward the light of common feeling. No one rests without expression, for man, striving to realize himself, works to master means and to find occasion to declare his selfhood. And all seek avidly for witnesses and hearers. Inveterately searching out experiences, enlarging perception, seeking expression, men are drawn together. Our deepest solidarities and mutualities perhaps arise out of the search for revelation and appreciation. Through such bonds are selves enlarged.

Imagine all men's work as art, though less than great. The artist's discipline provides a fair analogy to everyone's. The matter is expression. Expression needs a theme and subject, a consistent style, a unity. It calls for mastering a medium and for careful composition of each work or act. It rests on faithfulness to vision. Eventually it has to take account of its anticipated spectators, their tastes and depths. And thus, like artists, ordinary men must ponder and select, and practice and develop, their expression. Sensitivity toward environment, both physical and social, obviously plays its part herein. Perhaps a man shows fully *who* he is only when he clearly understands *where* he is. Most, living out their span in some small ambit, never much reflect and never question, but some who dare to look more deeply find a more rewarding way of declaration. These latter leave, in turn, the greater guidance for succeeding ages.

The possible repertories of self revelation are as varied as the selves. One man seeks to innovate, another glories in conformity. Either tradition or novelty will do. But all in all, the scope allowed to each of us is narrow; our initiatives will only slightly change the world. The total panorama of lands and cultures shows men almost entirely fixed within the orbits of their own inherited environments, participating in the only worlds conceivable to them. Reality begins at home.

The world, so full of change, astonishes by changing little. Ideas and institutions, seeming to conquer, only spread like desert cloudbursts, briefly raging, then sinking invisible into the soil. The homely fact of mere location, in the last analysis, counts more than all communication for the earth-rooted human species. But those flowerings of the spirit, the occasional great deeds, the noble thoughts, the greatest works of art, deny the lesson: they yet insist that man is free.

Geography, indeed, can document that peoples never merely capitulate to environments. Indomitably, they work to change. They seek expression, individual and corporate. And through expression they seek union.

But although change proceeds along forever, its trend is always toward diversity. Convergence and conformity in human ways have been historically, ephemeral achievements. Locality prevails. As their bonds become more intimate, environments and peoples, like old partners to a marriage, turn jointly more and more peculiar, and almost more and more alike.

And if peoples never kowtow altogether to environments, that side of peoples that is social environment can never master individuality. If uniformity advances so that anything original or individual becomes unwelcome deviance, then that very deviance may well be seized upon as vehicle for authentic selfhood—and communion. Self seeks difference. The hold of the community on its members, again, succumbs to urgent self-assertion. The very intercourse that binds societies inspires a jostling restlessness. And geographical contagion among cultures and societies puts in peril any stable system. Even more so, the universal fact of aggressive cultural and political expansion guarantees that no society can escape change. A cultural cycle forever repeats itself. Quiescence gives way somewhere to turbulence. An irresistible and dauntless leader arises, marshals his people, and sets out to conquer or convert the world. His movement sweeps over continents and overwhelms established states. But soon the force is spent, and under tranquil conditions the silent strength of local interest and sentiment dismembers the momentary unity and reverses much of the change achieved. Pulsating cycles of conquest and change, throughout history, have alternated with long quiet. Two modes of the cultural process occur: the one explosive and often ephemeral, the other slowly flowing on and soaking deep.

Geography records the expressions of men transforming environments, calling entire peoples into being. The palimpsest of earth preserves the traces of untold assertions of the human will and spirit, one inscription on another, half illegible. Deciphered even tentatively (for that is all their state permits), they restore a tale of culture living, moving, growing through communication.

Unity (*cont.*)
  mankind, 2, 82, 83, 99, 101
  person, 45
  place, 81

V

Values:
  art and, 76
  environment and, 44
  institutional, 44
  nation and, 41, 53, 89–91, 92, 93–
    94
Variation (*see* Differentiation)
Vitality, 2, 3, 41, 44, 56

W

War:
  communication and, 39, 94
  zones, 39
Way of life:
  ideal, in city, 48
  natural selection, 67–68
  settlement, 45–46, 48, 57–59, 69,
    82
Words, dispersal of, 21–22

Z

Zoroastrianism, 33–34